As one of the world's longest established
and best-known travel brands,
Thomas Cook are the experts in travel.

For more than 135 years our
guidebooks have unlocked the secrets
of destinations around the world,
sharing with travellers a wealth of
experience and a passion for travel.

**Rely on Thomas Cook as your
travelling companion on your next trip
and benefit from our unique heritage.**

Thomas Cook **traveller** guides

SOUTHWEST FRANCE

Jane Anson

Thomas Cook

Your travelling companion since 1873

Introduction

For an area that offers beaches, surfing, skiing, mountain walking, vibrant city life and world-renowned food and wines, southwest France is surprisingly often overlooked. It is slow France, hidden France, full of lazy corners where you can still walk for hours without meeting a single other person, or find beaches that have seemingly endless silver sands without a single footprint.

The area contains two of France's most dynamic cities in Toulouse and Bordeaux (respectively the fourth and fifth largest in the country, with around two million inhabitants between them), both with countless museums, restaurants and shopping opportunities. Yet even in these cities things shut down for a two-hour lunch break, and Sundays remain a day for relaxing with family and friends around a table laden with food and wine, or for getting outside and playing tennis, rugby, sailing... whatever the season and the scenery allows.

Southwest France celebrates the outdoors. Urban areas occupy just under 18 per cent of the overall land area, leaving vast expanses of natural spaces, and water is an ever-present influence on the landscape. The three great rivers of the Garonne, the Dordogne and the Lot meander their way from the French Pyrénées or the Massif Central mountain ranges to meet the Atlantic Ocean. Countless smaller rivers and lakes run alongside or into them, and the Canal du Midi remains an essential waterway – although primarily today for tourist traffic. All of this attracts some of the world's best surfers to the coastal resorts of Biarritz and Hossegor, where annual competitions host increasing numbers each year. Other attractions include Europe's highest sand dune at Pyla, near to Arcachon Bay, prehistoric cave paintings at several underground grottoes in the Dordogne, and also one of the world's most visited shrines at Lourdes, near Pau in the Hautes-Pyrénées. The soul of France could be said to be found in the mounds of fresh strawberries, asparagus, melons and tomatoes in markets that are held throughout the summer months across the smart market towns and bastides of the Gers and the Lot, while the sights, smells and tastes take on spicier overtones, with tiny red peppers strung up alongside smoked meats and hams, as you edge further down towards the Spanish border.

Perhaps all of this explains why the population of the southwest is at times fiercely proud of its regional identity. The Basque region that spans both the southwest tip of France and the northeast tip of Spain has not only its own language, but also its own foods, architecture and cultural institutions. And you'll find the majority of the locals from all over the southwest spending their summers on the Atlantic Coast rather than heading across country to the Côte d'Azur. And it's no surprise that the wine-drinkers here for the most part shun the international varieties, many of which spread from Bordeaux to California, Australia and Argentina but had less luck travelling a few kilometres down the road to Madiran, Irouléguy and Gaillac, where the winemakers instead celebrate their own indigenously grown varieties.

Introduction

A farmer tends his geese and guinea fowl

The region

Southwest France is seen as the 'Other South of France', covering the large areas of Aquitaine and the Midi-Pyrénées/Pyrénées-Atlantiques with 12 départements in total: Gironde, Dordogne, Lot, Tarn, Tarn-et-Garonne, Haute-Garonne, Ariège, Hautes-Pyrénées, Pyrénées-Atlantiques, Landes, Gers and the Lot-et-Garonne. Each département has its own flavour and pace of life, but the region as a whole is clearly delineated by significant natural boundaries.

This beautiful part of France is cut off by the Atlantic Ocean to the west, the tip of the Médoc peninsula and the Dordogne area to the north, the French Pyrénées to the south, and the foothills of the Massif Central to the east.

Dordogne and the Lot

These two regions, blanketed with lush trees and filled with steeply rising mountain roads, dramatic gorges, hilltop villages and the wide Dordogne and Lot rivers, have been attracting

The Dordogne river below Beynac

Pornic Vertou Cholet D960 Chinon Valençay Vierzon
Challans D753 Thouars Loudun Issoudun Bourges
A83 N149 D938 D347 D910 Clion D943 A20 St Amand-
La Roche- Les Bressuire Châtellerault D20 Montrond
sur-Yon Herbiers A10 Chateauroux La Châtre
D160 Fontenay- N149 Poitiers Le D951 La Châtre A71
Les-Sables le-Comte Parthenay N147 Blanc St-Marcel D943 Montluçon
d'Olonne D743 Coupé La D940 N145
Pertuis Breton D137 Niort VIENNE Souterraine
La Rochelle D137 La Rochelle DEUX- Charroux HAUTE Creuse Guéret
Pertuis d'Antioche SEVRES Charroux N145 CREUSE
St-Denis D137 St Jean- Ruffec Confolens VIENNE Ahun D942
-d'Oléron d'Angély D950 St-Junien St-Léonard- Aubusson
Rochefort A837 Matha CHARENTE Limoges de-Noblat D941
CHARENTE LIMOGES Eymoutiers
MARITIME Saintes N10 N141 Vienne
Royan Soyaux Parc Nexon Rogeat
Cognac N141 Régional Chålus St Yrieix la Perche Ussel
Le-Verdon-sur-Mer A10 N10 D939 Périgord Thiviers A20 D940 A89
St-Vivien- Combiers Limousin D707 CORRÈZE
de-Médoc Montlieu- Brantôme Périgueux Tulle Mauriac
Cavignac la-Garde Ribérac Isle A89 Brive-la- Murat
Bay of D674 Périgueux Thenon Gaillarde D922
Biscay GIRONDE D674 La Roche-Chalais DORDOGNE Souillac Martel CANTAL
Blanquefort Libourne Ste-Foy- Bergerac D57 Rocamadour Aurillac
St-Médard-en-Jalles la-Grande Domme Gramat D920
Bordeaux BORDEAUX Bergerac Parc Régional D122 Espalion
Cap Ferret D933 des Causses Cahors D840 AVEYRON
Arcachon Cestas St-Macaire N21 Mozeyrolles du Quercy Limogne Rodez
A63 Belin- A62 Fumel Villeneuve- LOT Villefranche- D911
Gujan Béliet Bazas sur-Lot LOT- de-Rouergue
Mestras D652 Moustey D3 Captieux Agen Lalbenque Villefranche- Carmaux
Ychoux Parc Régional Houeillès Moissac A20 Montauban Gaillac Parc Régional des
Solférino des Landes Sabres Roquefort Castelsarrasin D927 Albi Grands Causses
Miquéou de Gascogne D933 Condom TARN- Gaillac D999
N10 N134 Mont-de-Marsan GARONNE Graulhet
LANDE Tartas N124 D930 Auch TARN
D947 Adour Hagetmau Dému GERS Toulouse A62 TOULOUSE Castres
A63 Dax D947 D933 D834 D935 N124 Ramonville- Mazamet
Biarritz Bayonne Orthez Masseube Plaisance St-Agne D612
Salies-de- A64 Pau du-Touch D820 Castelnaudary
St-Jean- Béarn Tarbes N21 D929 Auterive A61 D610
de-Luz PYRÉNÉES- Pau HAUTE- A66 Carcassonne
St-Jean-Pied- ATLANTIQUES Tarbes GARONNE Pamiers D613
de-Port Oloron- Lourdes St-Gaudens Vals Mirepoix AUDE
Urcula Ste-Marie HAUTES- N125 Montels Ginoles
1419 D919 PYRÉNÉES Bosost ARIÈGE Niaux Estagel
Forca Parc National Luz-St- Mont Rouch Les Ax-les-Thermes
Pamplona 2390 des Pyrénées Sauveur Pic Cabannes Prades
A136 du-Part-d'Oo Coma Pic Carlit D118
N121 Liédena N240 Biescas Bielsa 2853 3114 Pedrosa N2 Porta 2921 Pic de Arles-sur-
A127 Pico d'Aneto e 2865 Puigcerdà la Vache Tech
Jaca N330 N260 3404 2946 2861 Camprodon
A132 Punta de Guara Pont Torre de Cadi N20
Sádaba 2078 de Suert N260 2567 Berga Girona
Ejea Huesca Barbastro Tremp Girona
Alagón A127 Monzón N230 N C16 C17
AP60 Zaragoza SPAIN A23 A131 N240 C26 C25 AP7
N230 Cervera Manresa

○ City
◉ Large Town
○ Small Town
Motorway
Main Road
Minor Road
✈ Airport
Railway
Regional Border
International Border

Château d'Yquem, creator of some of the world's finest wines

visitors for generations. A stay here should allow time for the exploration of cave paintings etched by prehistoric man and the perusal of duck-laden menus on riverside terraces. The main cities are Bergerac, Périgueux and Cahors, each hosting numerous food, music and art festivals throughout the busy summer period. Just south of the Lot, the Gers (also known as Gascony) has fields of sunflowers that are reminiscent of Provence, its bastide towns and its Armagnac presses.

Gironde

Just to the east of the Dordogne, the Gironde is home to both the city and the wine of Bordeaux. Vines hold sway here, and a drive around the area reveals row after row of them, setting off over 8,000 wine estates, from stately châteaux to simple cottages with outside wine vats. The Gironde also contains three UNESCO World Heritage Sites in the form of Blaye Citadel, the medieval village of Saint-Émilion and the culturally vibrant city of Bordeaux itself.

Lot-et-Garonne and Les Landes

This is the heart of rural southwest France, with France's largest pine forest clinging to the side of the coast and spreading over 10,000sq km (3,850sq miles) of protected parkland. The Lot-et-Garonne is often called the fruitbasket of the southwest, and you will find countless markets offering local artichokes, strawberries, melons, prunes and tomatoes. If you are after something a bit richer on

Statue of D'Artagnan, Auch, Gascony

the palate, you don't need to go far: this area is also the heart of the ubiquitous duck products, from rillettes to foie gras.

Toulouse and Tarn

As France slips down towards Spain, southwest France takes on a more 'southern' feel, with red-brick houses in Toulouse and Albi, fiestas held throughout the summer months, even bullfighting in the town of Mont-de-Marsan. Toulouse is one of France's most vibrant cities, with a large student population and a lively bar and restaurant scene. Temperatures are higher here, as you are further from the Atlantic Ocean, but you're rewarded by easy access to the beautiful scenery of Gaillac and Fronton and the mountain resorts of the Pyrénées and the Ariège region.

Pyrénées-Atlantiques

As the mountains of the Pyrénées approach, the landscape becomes more rugged and spectacular, and the architecture takes on the distinct white-and-red look of the Basque region. This is wonderful walking and driving country, with discoveries such as the hillside town of Saint-Jean-Pied-de-Port, and larger towns such as Pau and Lourdes. In the winter months, snow blankets the highest ground and the ski resorts swing into life, while in the summer, spa towns offer balneotherapy for beauty-seekers and for walkers returning from hillside treks.

A typical house in the Landes

The Garonne by night, Toulouse

History

15,000– 13,000 BC	Cro-Magnon man settles in the region of what will become Aquitaine. The caves of Lascaux in the Dordogne, together with many other sites in the Dordogne and Lot valleys, contain some of the earliest-known cave paintings, dating from between 17,000 and 15,000 years ago.
1st century	The Romans conquer Aquitania after defeating the Celts. The Pax Romana that follows is the start of the creation and growth of centres of commerce such as Burdigala (which became Bordeaux), Versunna (Périgueux) and Aginum (Agen).
1154	Eleanor of Aquitaine marries Henry II of England, and the region of Aquitaine becomes part of the English Crown. Bordeaux wines become one of its main exports.
1453	Battle of Castillon sees the English lose to the French forces, and Aquitaine returns to France.

1500s	During the Wars of Religion, Aquitaine becomes a Protestant stronghold. Many of the bastide towns are strengthened and key fortresses and citadels built.
1660	Marie Theresa, Infanta of Spain, marries Louis XIV in Saint-Jean-de-Luz. The wedding presents are pretty good: Cardinal Mazarin presents the queen with the equivalent of £12,000 of pearls and diamonds, a gold dinner service and a pair of sumptuous carriages drawn by teams of six horses.
1700s	Bordeaux becomes centre of trade for spices, coffee, sugar and wine, which are sent from the city's port out to the French colonies and the Americas.
1789	In the French Revolution, Bordeaux's Place Gambetta sees 300 aristocrats led to the guillotine.
1850s	Empress Eugénie and the court of Napoleon III make Biarritz a favourite tourist spot by spending their

summers there enjoying the thermal waters. The emperor has a large villa built on the water; the villa will later become the Hotel du Palais.

1855 Bordeaux wines are classified during the Paris Exhibition, thus beginning the world's most famous wine-ranking system that still holds sway today.

1914 The government of France moves briefly to Bordeaux at the start of World War I.

1920s Toulouse builds the Latecoere aircraft factory, beginning France's airmail service.

1930s This is the decade when the southwest of France lays claim to being France's aviation centre. One of the flying world's first famous women, aviator Hélène Boucher, practises her flying skills in Mont-de-Marsan. At the same time, the famous aircraft La Croix du Sud, flown by Mermoz, comes out of the factory in Biscarrosse, and the Société Nationale de Construction Aéronautique du Sud-Ouest, later to become Dassault, develops its activities.

1940 Charles de Gaulle flies from Merignac airport in Bordeaux to London to begin the Free France movement.

1992 Queen Elizabeth II visits Bordeaux and declares, 'I am delighted to visit this French city, which is the very essence of elegance'.

2006 Bordeaux is granted UNESCO World Heritage status.

2011 Work is scheduled to begin on a high-speed rail link, cutting journey times from Bordeaux and Toulouse to Paris and Madrid by one hour. The line is expected to open in 2016.

2013 The Wine Cultural Centre is due to open in Bordeaux.

2016 Both Toulouse and Bordeaux will host football matches in the European Championships.

2020 Toulouse is expected to become the third-largest city in France, behind Paris and Marseille.

Politics

Southwest France is part of mainland metropolitan France and so is governed by President Nicolas Sarkozy and his UMP (Union pour un Mouvement Populaire, or Union for a Popular Movement) government. As with the rest of France, it is also part of the European Union, and so many of its laws and policies come from both Paris and Brussels.

There is, however, a thriving local political scene, reflective of the importance that Bordeaux and Toulouse have both been accorded over the centuries (the French government even briefly relocated to Bordeaux during World Wars I and II). Aquitaine and the Midi-Pyrénées have a regional council comprised of a number of local councillors drawn from various political parties including Les Verts (The Greens), the Parti Socialiste (Socialist Party), the UMP and the UDF (Union pour la Démocratie Française, or Union for French Democracy). The regional council has legislative power at a local level and represents the interests of the region at a national level. The president of this regional council in Aquitaine, based in Bordeaux, is Alain Rousset. The equivalent for the Midi-Pyrénées is Martin Malvy, based in Toulouse.

The two regional capital cities also have elected mayors who have a clear influence on the local political scene.

In Bordeaux, Mayor Alain Juppé is a former prime minister of France and has been credited with reviving the city centre, being able to push through a raft of improvements and renovation projects due to his continued strong influence in Paris. He was elected mayor in 2006, and remains there despite a brief return to Paris in 2007 as Minister of State for Sustainable Development (and continued rumours that he is due to return to the main political scene). In Toulouse, Pierre Cohen has been mayor since 2008 and has also presided over extensive renovation projects, particularly of the transport infrastructure.

Outside of the main areas of population, politics are felt most passionately in the Basque region. The inhabitants of this beautiful part of the country feel their own separate identity very strongly, and road signs are most usually displayed in both the Basque language and in French. The Basque flag was created in 1894 by Sabino Arana, the founder of Basque nationalism. The name of the flag is *ikurriña*, and it is usually flown alongside the French flag outside town halls and mayors' offices in the many towns and villages of the French Pyrénées.

The local press is also strong, led by the Sud Ouest newspaper group which covers the entire region and is the third-largest regional publication in France, with a circulation of around 300,000. Created in Bordeaux in 1944, today it has different editions across the Gironde, the Charente, the Charente-Maritime, the Dordogne, the Pyrénées-Atlantiques and the Lot-et-Garonne, covering a mixture of local and national news. The president of the group is Pierre Jeantet, who has been in this role since February 2008. Eighty per cent of the group belong to the Lemoine family, 10 per cent to the journalists, and the remaining 10 per cent to the staff. This is an excellent source for coverage of local politics and current affairs, and national events are often related through the context of their effects on southwest France.

Campaign posters, Bordeaux

Regional specialities: Bayonne ham

There are few better ways to get to know southwest France than through seeing the care and attention that goes into preparing its local foods. This area of France abounds with artisan producers, often upholding centuries-old traditions, or rescuing ones that were close to dying out. Bayonne ham is a great example of this. A cured ham that has similarities to Italian *prosciutto* or Spanish *serrano* ham, it has a history that dates from the 11th century. Until the late 1990s, however, the use of the name had spread far beyond the region and had ceased to be linked to a specific method of production. But the French are vigilant when it comes to protecting their culinary heritage, and by 1988, sufficient pressure had been exerted by local producers to result in it being given both an IGP (Indication Géographique Protégée) and its own governing body – **Le Consortium de Jambon du Bayonne** (*www.jambon-de-bayonne.fr*) – based in Pau.

The city of Bayonne – with just 40,000 inhabitants in its downtown area – is synonymous with ham (it even holds a festival in its honour every Easter). Since it was given an IGP, the rules governing its production are clear. The meat itself does not have to come from the Adour basin but has to be produced from one of

Bayonne

eight clearly defined breeds of pig reared in an area that reaches from Deux Sèvres in the north to Aveyron and the Aude – basically wider southwest France. The regulations are very strict and cover the zone of origin of the pork, the regime for feeding the animals (no steroids, no fish oils, no antibiotics), and each animal must be clearly and uniquely identifiable with a tattoo.

To make true *jambon de Bayonne*, fresh hams are rubbed and covered with salt from the Adour basin, then put into a salting tub. After several days they are washed to remove the excess salt, and sometimes pressed if they are too wet. Finally, the hams are hung in a curing room, where they lose some of their weight and slowly dry. It takes from nine to twelve months to cure a Bayonne ham. Local producers assert that it is not only this slow drying process but also the local breezes, finely salted from the nearby Atlantic Ocean, that contribute to the flavour. Bigger producers today may use air-conditioning units to ensure air circulates continually around the hams, while small producers depend on natural draughts, so look out for open windows intended to catch the winds.

To verify the authenticity of a ham, look for the *Lauburu* (the Basque cross) marked on the rind with a

Espelette peppers are used to flavour the ham

branding iron. Two high-quality firms to visit are Pierre Ibaïalde (*41 rue des Cordeliers, Bayonne. Tel: 05 59 25 65 30. www.pierre-ibaialde.com*) and Maison Montauzer (*17 rue de la Salle, Bayonne. Tel: 05 59 59 07 68*). When in Bayonne, you can also just head down to the market along the River Nive, where you'll find lots of small stalls selling hams alongside other regional foodstuffs. And once you've procured your prized ham, one of the best ways to serve it includes thinly slicing it to eat either on its own or paired with fresh melon. It is also used as an ingredient in much Basque cooking, often with chicken or salted cod. And look out for hams that have used the spicy red peppers from the Basque village of Espelette in their production process – these have a gentle kick that is utterly delicious.

Culture

Culture in southwest France spans everything from operas, ballets and musicals at the Grand Théâtre in Bordeaux or the Théâtre du Capitole in Toulouse, to tomato festivals in Marmande, prune festivals in Agen and the legendary jazz festival in Marciac. Legends and great literature abound in this richly textured corner of France, none more lasting than that of Les Trois Mousquetaires *(The Three Musketeers).*

This famous work was written first as a novel by Alexandre Dumas in the 19th century, but set 200 years earlier and apparently based on memoirs of a lieutenant-captain of Louis XIV's army (although in the book the king is Louis XIII). Much of the plot is based around towns in the Gers, and visitors will still see references to the stories in street names, cafés, books and films when travelling around the region. A more recent novel set in the region is *Chocolat* by Joanne Harris, where the characters open a chocolate shop in a village 'somewhere between Toulouse and Bordeaux'. *The Matchmaker of Perigord*, by Julia Stuart, was published in 2008 and is also set in an imaginary village in southwest France.

Besides the two main centres of Toulouse and Bordeaux – which between them have over 20 art galleries, 30 museums and dozens of large and small concert venues – there are several other key cultural centres in the region, including Périgueux, Bergerac, Biarritz, Albi and Pau. All of these have their own thriving cultural scene and play host to several festivals throughout the year. Cahors is home to numerous venues, and hosts regular cultural events. The renowned mime artist (and a powerful figure in the French Resistance during World War II) Marcel Marceau died in Cahors, where he spent the last years of his life, and the city hosts several exhibitions and events dedicated to him. His daughter Aurelia is an actress and often performs in theatres in the region. Toulouse was home to Antoine de Saint-Exupéry, best known as the author of *Le Petit Prince*, and you can expect to see his name on streets and cafés all over the city – just as Stendhal, De Montesquieu and François Mauriac reign supreme in Bordeaux, and Toulouse-Lautrec will be forever associated with Albi. The annual Marathon des Mots festival in Toulouse invites today's writers, artists and essayists to host readings and workshops and celebrate the written word. Even Shakespeare is celebrated – in English – over the summer months, when the Quercy players stage shows all over the Lot region (*see p155*).

You might also find that certain locations around southwest France seem a little familiar, even on your first visit. The reason is that many of the castles and romantic cobbled towns and villages have been used as film sets over the years, such as Beynac in the Dordogne, which was used for the opening scenes of the 2000 film *Chocolat*, or Sarlat and the Château de Hautefort (also in the Dordogne) in the 1998 film *Ever After*. This may happen even more regularly in the future, as from 2009 the French government came in line with much of the rest of Europe and agreed to a 20 per cent tax rebate for foreign film productions shot in France.

Musée des Beaux-Arts, Agen

Festivals and events

Vibrant festivals and cultural events are held throughout the year in the different southwest regions, reflecting the many diverse cultures that live here. Several revolve around local foods and wines, others around regional history, and still others are simply excuses to celebrate. Wherever you plan to stay, always check the events calendar with the local tourist office and be prepared to change your plans to accommodate an interesting-sounding festival.

January–February
International Violet Festival: Toulouse is seen as the world capital of violets, and soaps, perfumes, sweets and drinks dedicated to this beautiful flower are found all over the city.

March–April
Printemps du Rire: Annual comedy festival held in various venues in Toulouse showcasing stand-up comedians, comic drama and musical comedy.
www.printempsdurire.com
Foire au Jambon: Each Easter, the city of Bayonne holds its annual festival celebrating Bayonne ham, the region's most famous export.
www.bayonne-tourisme.com

May–June
Le Week-end des Grands Amateurs: For one weekend in May, the region's top wine châteaux hold tastings for the general public in central Bordeaux, and offer visits and dinners in the prestigious properties.
www.wga-ugcb.com. Admission charge.
Bordeaux Fête le Vin: Once every two years (the next one is planned for June 2012), this attracts 500,000 visitors along the quays of Bordeaux to taste the local wines, talk to the winemakers and sample the local foods. A music and river festival is held at the same time.
www.bordeaux-fete-le-vin.com
Marathon des Mots: A literary festival held in Toulouse that brings writers and artists together for a series of workshops and readings.
www.lemarathondesmots.com

July–August
La Bataille de Castillon: The biggest and most decisive battle of the Hundred Years War took place at Castillon-la-Bataille. This battle saw the English driven out of the area and is celebrated today by huge events that are staged regularly through the summer months.
www.batailledecastillon.com

Jazz in Marciac: 2010 saw the 30th anniversary of the Marciac jazz festival, an event that regularly attracts the biggest names in the business. *www.jazzinmarciac.com. Admission charge.*

Les Grands Crus Musicaux: Classical music concerts are held in the grounds of prestigious châteaux around the Médoc. *www.grandscrusmusicaux.com*

Saveurs et Senteurs du Frontonnais (Flavours and Fragrances of Fronton): A big festival is held in Fronton on the last weekend of August (the bank holiday weekend in the UK). There's jazz and blues to keep you entertained and local producers of everything from foie gras to honey. *Fronton town centre, among various other locations. Tel: 05 61 82 46 33.*

Fêtes de la Madeleine: Mont-de-Marsan is the site of one of the region's most colourful festivals, covering two days (often extended by smaller events on either side) that usually fall on the last weekend of July. *www.fetesmadeleine.fr*

September–October

Les Jurades de Saint-Émilion: The grape harvest is celebrated with an annual street festival culminating in fireworks over the medieval streets of this pretty town on the third Saturday of September.

La Fête du Piment: The Espelette Pepper Festival takes place in the last weekend of October and is a riot of colour, with garlands of the tiny red peppers strung outside houses and endless stalls selling local food, wine and other goodies. *www.pimentdespelette.com*

November–December

Toulouse jazz nights: La Maison Midi-Pyrénées hosts evenings throughout autumn and winter where visitors can go for a walk to different attractions followed by a jazz festival. *La Maison Midi-Pyrénées, 1 rue Rémusat, Toulouse. Tel: 05 34 44 18 18.*

Christmas markets: These are held around the region, including on the Allées de Tourny in Bordeaux and the Place du Capitole in Toulouse. For a more unusual Christmas experience, try the tiny village of Castelmoron-d'Albret to the south of Bordeaux (the smallest commune in France), where Nativity scenes are set up around the picturesque streets and in windows of village houses.

Les Vendanges de Saint Sylvestre: A late wine harvest in Saint Mont, harvested on December 31 and always celebrated by a festival. This is centred around the village of Viella in the Gers, and offers a gourmet food market and various entertainments. *www.plaimont.com*

TOURIST INFORMATION

There is a new number within France to ring and get any tourist board you want. Just call 3264 (€0.34 euro/min), and clearly say the place that you want. You will be put through automatically.

Highlights

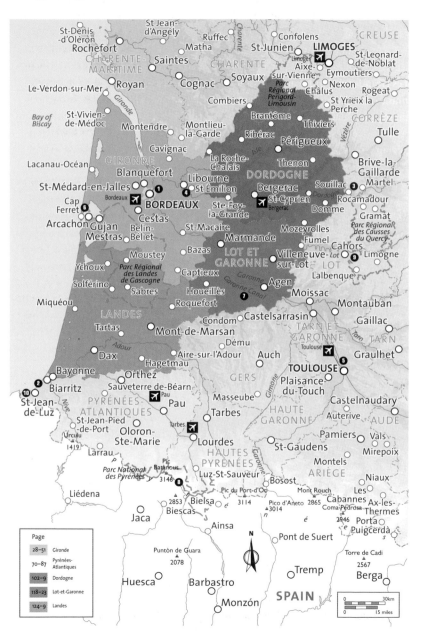

St-Denis-d'Oléron
Rochefort
St Jean-d'Angély
Ruffec
Matha
Confolens
St-Junien
LIMOGES
CREUSE
CHARENTE-MARITIME
Saintes
CHARENTE
Aixe-Sur-Vienne
Eymoutiers
St-Leonard-de-Noblat
Le-Verdon-sur-Mer
Royan
Cognac
Soyaux
Parc Régional Périgord-Limousin
Châlus
Nexon
St Yrieix la Perche
Rogeat
Bay of Biscay
St-Vivien-de-Médoc
Montendre
Combiers
Brantôme
Thiviers
CORRÈZE
Tulle
Montlieu-la-Garde
Ribérac
Périgueux
Cavignac
La Roche-Chalais
Thenon
Brive-la-Gaillarde
Lacanau-Océan
GIRONDE
Blanquefort
Libourne
DORDOGNE
Souillac
Martel
St-Médard-en-Jalles
St Émilion
Bergerac
St-Cyprien
Bergerac
Rocamadour
Cap Ferret
Bordeaux
BORDEAUX
Ste-Foy-la-Grande
Domme
Gramat
Arcachon
Gujan-Mestras
Cestas
Belin-Béliet
St-Macaire
Mozeyrolles
Parc Régional des Causses du Quercy
Ychoux
Moustey
Bazas
Marmande
Fumel
Cahors
Villeneuve-sur-Lot
LOT
Limogne
Solférino
Parc Régional des Landes de Gascogne
Captieux
LOT ET GARONNE
Garonne Canal
Agen
Lalbenque
Miquéou
Sabres
Houeillès
Moissac
Tartas
Roquefort
LANDES
Condom
Castelsarrasin
Montauban
Mont-de-Marsan
Dému
Gaillac
TARN ET GARONNE
Dax
Adour
Aire-sur-l'Adour
Auch
Toulouse
TARN
Graulhet
Bayonne
Orthez
Hagetmau
GERS
Plaisance-du-Touch
TOULOUSE
Biarritz
Sauveterre-de-Béarn
Pau
Masseube
Castelnaudary
St-Jean-de-Luz
PYRÉNÉES-ATLANTIQUES
Pau
Tarbes
HAUTE GARONNE
Auterive
AUDE
St-Jean-Pied-de-Port
Oloron-Ste-Marie
Tarbes
Pamiers
Vals
Urculu 1419
Larrau
Lourdes
St-Gaudens
Mirepoix
Liédena
Parc National des Pyrénées
Pic Batanous 3146
HAUTES PYRÉNÉES
Luz-St-Sauveur
Montels
ARIÈGE
Niaux
Bosost
Les
Pic du Port-d'Oo
Mont Rouch
2853
Bielsa
3114
Pico d'Aneto 2865
Cabannes
Ax-les-Thermes
Jaca
Biescas
3014
Coma Pédrosa
Porta
Ainsa
2946
Puigcerdà
N
Punton de Guara 2078
Torre de Cadi 2567
Pont de Suert
Huesca
Barbastro
Tremp
Berga
Monzón
SPAIN

0   30km
0   15 miles

1 **Cooling your feet in the Miroir d'Eau** The UNESCO World Heritage city of Bordeaux is full of graceful 18th-century buildings, but one of its best attractions is entirely more recent (*see p36*).

2 **Surfing in Biarritz** The Atlantic Coast offers some of the best surfing opportunities in France, where the Bay of Biscay channels wave after wave to happy surfers (*see pp58–9*).

3 **Wandering through the perched villages of the Dordogne** Sun-baked 2,000-year-old stone walls, dizzying views over surrounding cracked rocks with peaks of green-tufted grasses and trees, cicadas slowly singing, dusty streets giving way to welcome shady squares, occasional glimpses of the silver-backed Dordogne river... (*see pp105–7*).

4 **Going underground in Saint-Émilion** Classified as a UNESCO World Heritage Site since 1999, this is one of the must-see destinations in the Bordeaux vineyards (*see p36*).

5 **Exploring the Cité de L'Espace in Toulouse** The Space City amusement park and science centre celebrates Toulouse's connection with space and aviation with some terrific interactive exhibits (*see p90*).

6 **Slurping oysters in Cap Ferret** A short drive from the city of Bordeaux, this effortless resort is all about wooden oyster huts, empty beaches, and countless seafood restaurants that look out over the gently sloping Bassin d'Arcachon (*see pp54–5*).

7 **Boating down the Canal de Garonne** Follow the canal as it flows 104km (65 miles) from Castets-en-Dorthe down to Saint-Romaine-le-Noble, passing 22 locks along the way (*see p122*).

8 **Hiking through the Pays Basque** The Pyrénées, forming a craggy barrier between France and Spain, reach an average height of 1,600m (5,250ft) and offer plenty of hiking opportunities (*see pp158–9*).

9 **Truffle-hunting in Cahors** In Cahors and the surrounding villages, truffle markets are held during the winter months, and fierce bidding goes on for the 'Black Diamond of Quercy' (*see p102*).

10 **Indulging at the gourmet weekend in Saint-Jean-de-Luz** Perhaps it's the Spanish passion that permeates every corner of this beautiful Basque resort, or perhaps it's the French feel for pastries and desserts, but Saint-Jean-de-Luz has become one of the leading foodie destinations in the southwest (*see pp64–5*).

Suggested itineraries

Long weekend

Bordeaux and Arcachon

With four days to explore the southwest, head straight to the city of Bordeaux. You won't need a car for this, as the public transport system around the city is very good, and a local train can take you either east out to the village of Saint-Émilion, or west to the Atlantic Coast and the pretty coastal resort of Arcachon and the Dune de Pyla. Make sure that you visit the historic city centre of Bordeaux, much of which is pedestrianised, as well as the vibrant quays along the river Garonne. There are good markets on the quays on both Thursday and Sunday, and cafés, jogging paths and playgrounds provide delightful diversions the rest of the week. The downside of this itinerary is missing out on the more exotic flavour of Toulouse and the French Basque region, but you can at least head to one of the many Basque-style restaurants in Bordeaux to get a flavour of what the wider region has to offer.

Saint-Émilion

The Assezat, Toulouse

One week
From Bergerac through the Dordogne, the Lot and Toulouse

With one week, you could consider flying into Bergerac rather than Bordeaux (by train, however, it is probably quickest to head to the major stations of Bordeaux or Toulouse, as these are served by the TGV, and then take local trains around the rest of the region). Once there, spend a few days exploring the cliff-top villages of the Dordogne, such as Souillac and Domme, then travel down through the Lot, checking out the medieval streets of Cahors, and the beautiful riverside villages of Puy-l'Evêque and Carennac. You could take a winding route down to Toulouse, where you can balance the beautiful countryside that you have just passed through with a vibrant few days of city life. When there, make sure you don't miss Les Abattoirs art museum, or the aeronautical delights of the Cité de l'Espace.

Two weeks
One week in Bordeaux and the vineyards, followed by a drive down the Atlantic Coast

For two weeks, it is best to hire a car to really explore the area fully, as when you head out from the major population centres, public transport can become more sporadic. Spend the first week in city and vineyard mode

Pepper-strewn hotel in Espelette

(you could even visit the three UNESCO World Heritage Sites of Bordeaux, Saint-Émilion and the Citadel de Blaye), then shift down a gear and get into the beach vibe along the Atlantic Coast road, from Arcachon down to Biarritz and Saint-Jean-de-Luz. As you head down towards the Basque region, make sure you try out the regional specialities of Brébis cheese, Espelette peppers and Bayonne ham, and don't miss the opportunity to try out a little surfing along the way. Every beach resort along the coast will have a surf school where you can take lessons ranging in length from just a few hours to a week-long intensive session. If you prefer to stay on dry land, head up into the French Pyrénées for some serious walking.

Longer

With three weeks or longer, you can really get to know southwest France slowly. Start at the northern tip of the region, with Bordeaux and the Médoc vineyards, then head over to Bergerac, Périgueux and the Dordogne. This time, when travelling down through the Lot, ensure you spend a few days in

Cahors getting to know its vibrant cultural scene and its wonderful Malbec-based wines. Then keep heading further south and over to Albi, Gaillac and the stunning cliff-top town of Cordes-sur-Ciel. The Millau Viaduct – one of France's most famous landmarks ever since its opening in 2004 – is a little further east in the Aveyron region. Once you've explored all this, head over to Toulouse and on into the Basque region and the mountains of the Pyrénées.

Follow the Canal de Garonne south from Bordeaux

Bordeaux and vineyards

Bordeaux in recent years has become one of the most attractive and vibrant cities in France, throwing off its traditional image as a staid, buttoned-up kind of place where all anyone did was swirl, sniff and spit the local wine. There's still plenty of that of course, but the city today has a vibrant arts scene, a dedicated foodie vibe, plus a beautiful city centre.

Sitting snugly along a croissant-shaped fold in the Garonne river and with an almost entirely low-rise skyline, the UNESCO-protected Old Town has the highest number of classified monuments in France outside of Paris.

A sleek tram system, alongside the recent initiative of bicycle-hire stations around the city centre (just as in Paris and London), makes exploring extremely easy. And if you can't resist the wines, there are over 8,000

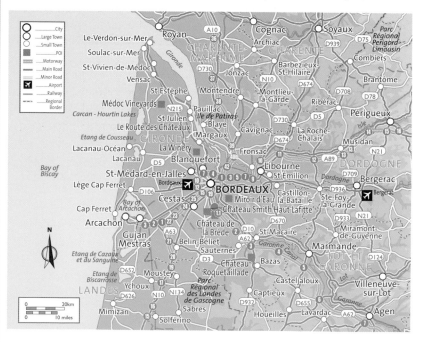

Place de la Bourse, Bordeaux

vineyards to explore in the surrounding areas (remember that the name Bordeaux applies to the city itself, the wine region that lies around it and the wine that is produced here). These range from tiny family-run estates to large glamorous châteaux, and increasingly offer far more to visitors than a simple cellar visit – you might find yourself today at an art exhibition, a farmers' market, or even helping out with the harvest.

Bordeaux city

Gone are the days when visitors to the region barely picked up their bags at the airport before heading out to the beach or the vines. Today, the city of Bordeaux deserves its own visit, whether for a city-break weekend or a longer stay. The city centre has excellent shopping and cultural opportunities, together with many great restaurants and an ever-expanding number of wine bars and wine shops for getting to grips with the local produce. And with a good-sized student population, even the nightlife has improved in recent years, and you'll find plenty of bars and clubs (although the city still has some way to go to equal Toulouse for post-midnight haunts).

Base Sous-Marine (Submarine Base)

An eerie but compelling place to visit, slightly off the usual tourist trail of Bordeaux. These hulking concrete buildings were submarine pens built between 1941 and 1943 by the Germans during World War II, and today some

Cathédrale Saint-André

1.2 hectares (3 acres) of the 4.2-hectare (10¼-acre) compound are open to the public. They contain an exhibition about the U-boats, together with regular art exhibitions, concerts and cultural events held throughout the year. This is one of the few intact examples of its kind, and as such has great historical importance. Around it, in the Bassins à Flot area of the city, is a marina that is due for extensive renovations over the next few years.
Boulevard Alfred Daney, 33300 Bordeaux. Tel: 05 56 11 11 50. Open: irregular hours, depending on exhibitions; call ahead. Admission charge for some exhibitions. Tram: Bassins à Flot.

Cathédrale Saint-André (Saint Andrew's Cathedral)

Set in a large paved square, this 13th-century cathedral is one of the city's most impressive sights, towering over the pavement cafés that surround it and renowned for its excellent stained-glass windows. Alongside it is the Tour Pey Berland, a bell tower that is open to the public. The town hall is located in the same square and is also worth a stroll round for its attractive central courtyard.
Place Pey Berland. Tel: 05 56 87 17 18. Open: Jun–Sept 10am–6pm; Oct–May 10am–noon & 2–5pm. Free admission. Tram: Hôtel de Ville.

Centre Jean Moulin

On the far side of place Pey Berland, this fascinating museum explores the Resistance forces during World War II and contains a collection of old propaganda posters used by the Nazis to encourage French cooperation. Resistance hero Jean Moulin and the role that Bordeaux played are given pride of place.

48 place Jean Moulin, rue Vital Carles. Tel: 05 56 79 66 00. Open: Tue–Fri 11am–6pm, Sat & Sun 2–6pm. Admission charge. Tram: Hôtel de Ville.

Chartrons

This traditional wine merchant district sits behind the Quai des Chartrons and is today a chic residential quarter. This is the best place to find well-stocked

Bordeaux's tram system makes getting around easy

Bordeaux and vineyards

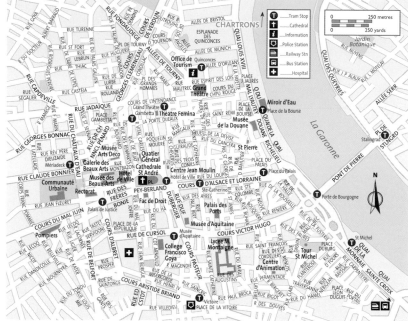

épiceries and interior-design stores, alongside a large antiques emporium and the very pretty rue de Fauberg des Arts. On rue Borie you'll find a small museum housed in an old vaulted cellar that looks at the history of the wine trade through its merchants, known as *négociants*. Heading a little further down towards the centre of town, you'll find the beautiful Jardin Public, the city's most central green space, on your right-hand side along cours Verdun.

Jardin Botanique (Botanical Garden)

On the *rive droite* is the area known as La Bastide. Place Stalingrad, with its huge blue lion statue, is a good place to start, but it's the ever-expanding green spaces that make for the best visit. The Jardin Botanique covers 1,500sq m (16,150sq ft) organised into distinct zones, from a water garden to a arboretum filled with trees more commonly found in the southern hemisphere.

Allées Jean Giono. Tel: 05 56 52 18 77. Open: summer 8am–10pm; winter 8am–6pm. Free admission. Tram: Stalingrad.

Musée d'Aquitaine (Aquitaine Museum)

This is a brilliant place in which to gain understanding of the history of the area, but also to look at modern-day Bordeaux and see what has shaped the

(*Cont. on p36*)

Porte Cailhau, Bordeaux

Walk: Through the UNESCO Old Town of Bordeaux

The enchanting Old Town of Bordeaux is easily covered on foot, and, as with most French cities, every other shop seems to be a welcoming café or restaurant.

The whole walk covers around 3km (nearly 2 miles) and should take two hours at a fast pace, although you're best to plan for at least half a day, and a full day if you want to explore all the museums and stop for a long lunch.

Start at the place de la Bourse and head directly inwards to the Old Town, taking the left-hand road that leads back from the square. If you have taken the train to Bordeaux, you can take the tram from directly outside the station and get off at the Bourse stop.

1 Place du Parlément

This pretty, cobbled square, with its central fountain, is full of bookshops and pavement cafés, together with a good ice-cream shop and plenty of people-watching opportunities.
Walk up rue de Pas Saint-Georges.

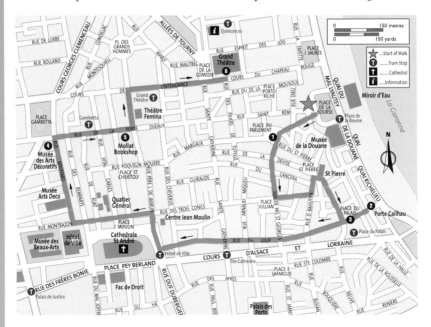

Cross over place Camille Jullian and head down rue Maucounidet towards Porte Cailhau.

2 Porte Cailhau

One of the few monuments in the city that has remained unchanged since medieval times, it is possible to climb to the top of the tower for a lovely view, but this must be arranged through the tourist office (*www.bordeaux-tourisme.com*).
Walk back into the place du Palais.

3 Place du Palais

Just behind the Porte Cailhau, this pretty square has been recently renovated.
Take rue du Loup towards place Pey Berland, stopping in at Saint-André cathedral (see p30) and the Centre Jean Moulin (see p31) before taking rue des Trois Conils up to rue Bouffard.

4 Musée des Arts Décoratifs (Decorative Arts Museum)

As you walk up past place Pey Berland (*see pp30–31*) into the antiques area of rue Bouffard, just on your left you'll see a lovely cobbled courtyard marking the entrance to this small, elegant museum.
39 rue Bouffard. Tel: 05 56 10 14 00. Open: Wed–Mon 2–6pm. Admission charge. Tram: Pey Berland.
Continue up rue Bouffard, stopping in at a few clothes, furniture and tea shops, to place Gambetta, and then turn right into the shopping street of rue de la Porte Dijeaux.

The view up rue du Loup

5 Mollat bookshop

This is Bordeaux's oldest family-run bookshop and one of the largest independent bookshops in France.
rue de la Porte Dijeaux. Open: Mon–Sat 9.30am–7pm. Tram: Sainte-Catherine.
Turn left on rue de Grassi onto cours de l'Intendance.

6 Grand Théâtre

Finish your walking tour at the neoclassical columns of the Grand Théâtre, designed by Victor Hugo and inaugurated in 1780, just a decade before the French Revolution.
To return to the starting point, turn right (when facing the Grand Théâtre) into rue Sainte-Catherine, then left onto rue Saint-Rémi, then right into the place du Parlément.

city to become the centre of wine it is today. You'll find everything from full-scale re-creations of Roman mosaic flooring to an unblinking exploration of the part that slavery played in the development of the city.

20 cours Pasteur.
Tel: 05 56 01 51 00. Open: Tue–Sun 11am–6pm. Free admission.
Tram: Musée d'Aquitaine.

Musée des Beaux-Arts (Museum of Fine Arts)

One of the most impressive buildings of all the city's museums, this 16th-century structure lies in the middle of the gardens of the *Hôtel de Ville* (town hall). It houses both permanent and temporary exhibitions, split over two galleries, including works by Rubens and Titian, and more modern artists such as Picasso and Dufy.

20 cours d'Albret. Tel: 05 56 96 61 50.
Open: Wed–Mon 11am–6pm. Free admission. Tram: Hôtel de Ville, then five minutes' walk.

Place de la Bourse and the Miroir d'Eau

The 3km (nearly 2 miles) of renovated quayside that runs along the Garonne river is lined with buildings that date back to a project begun by architect Jacques Gabriel in 1765, but the careful cleaning and renovation of the stone façades began just over a decade ago. Today you can join walkers, cyclists, skaters and joggers enjoying the wide paved walkway that contains parks, play

SAINT-ÉMILION'S UNDERGROUND MONUMENTS

Over the past centuries, the limestone hill on which Saint-Émilion sits has been the site of extensive quarries, used to extract blocks of stone to construct buildings in Saint-Émilion. Today, the subterranean landscape comprises a mixture of man-made limestone cellars (over 200km/124 miles of them) and natural caves (including the original grotto inhabited by the eponymous Émilion), the Trinity Chapel built in the saint's honour, the catacombs, a former underground cemetery and the monolithic church. There is even an underground pottery museum, the Musée Souterrain de la Poterie, which also sells pieces. (*Les Hospices de la Madeleine, 21 rue André Loiseau. Tel: 05 57 24 60 93. www.saint-emilion-museepoterie.fr. Open: daily 10am–6pm. Admission charge.*) The tourist office organises daily tours of the underground monuments.

areas, cafés, sports grounds and the beautiful Miroir d'Eau. This is 2,735sq m (29,440sq ft) of shallow water that serves as a reflective mirror of the Place de la Bourse, and a giant paddling pool for visitors and Bordelais of all ages. The water alternates between spray, jets and a shallow pool, and on sunny days seems to attract half the children of the city to run up and down in it. Designed by Parisian architect Jean-Max Llorca, this forms the focal point of the riverside, while the flowerbeds of the Jardin des Lumières surround it on either side.

Place de la Bourse. Free admission.
Tram: Place de la Bourse.

Monument aux Girondins

Saint-Pierre

Head to Saint-Pierre, the epicentre of Old Bordeaux, for street markets, a laid-back vibe and eclectic shopping in venues ranging from cool interior-design shops to one-off clothes stores. Hidden among its streets is a Gothic church that dates from the 15th century. This spot marks the exact site of the original Gallo-Roman port that grew into the city of Bordeaux.

Place Saint-Pierre. Tel: 05 56 52 24 68. Free admission. Tram: Place de la Bourse.

Floral display in an old wine-press

ELEANOR OF AQUITAINE

Today's Bordeaux wine lovers owe a special debt of gratitude to the turbulent love life of one particular woman who ruled southwest France nearly 1,000 years ago. Eleanor (or Alienor) of Aquitaine was one of the wealthiest and most powerful people in Europe during the Middle Ages, highly unusual at a time when men were pretty much regarded as the only show in town. She was also striking and spirited, and managed to create a few scandals by divorcing her first husband and then marrying a much younger man. The latter was not only her distant cousin, but also a man with serious prospects: he became King Henry II of England in 1154, not long after their marriage. As part of her dowry, Eleanor's lands in Aquitaine became part of the English Crown, and taxes were abolished on any goods travelling over the Channel. Wine was one of those things, and the steady influx of merchants and traders to the region, many of whom then bought land to grow vines themselves, helped to develop Bordeaux into the fine wine epicentre that it is today. The region also set up a system of trading Bordeaux wines – with a separate layer of merchants quite distinct from the people who made the wine – that continues to this day.

Saint-Émilion

The UNESCO World Heritage town of Saint-Émilion is one of the most visited sites in France. With a history that dates from the 8th century, it grew up as a religious site due to miracles performed by a monk called Émilion, who was originally from Brittany, but he chose this spot to devote his life to solitude and prayer. Even with the crowds that materialise on hot summer days, this is one of the unmissable destinations of

The *donjon* ('tower') of Saint-Émilion's 12th-century castle

the Bordeaux region and well worth at least half a day of your time. The town, located around 40km (25 miles) to the east of Bordeaux close to the Dordogne river and the attractive market town of Libourne, reveals its religious heritage through two particularly interesting churches, although it is now best known for its wine.

Besides the many châteaux to visit, there are also impossibly picturesque steeply cobbled streets (remember to wear low-heeled shoes, because climbing up and down these streets can be lethal on rainy days), an ancient *lavoir* (washing house) and numerous cafés, restaurants and bars alongside – of course – numerous wine shops. Saint-Émilion is a straightforward train ride from Bordeaux, and the small

LA WINERY

There is more to the Médoc than La Route des Châteaux, and this large wine and arts centre offers an alternative to visitors who take the straighter D1 road that heads directly up the centre of the peninsula to Le Verdon and the Point du Médoc. There is a large wine store that stocks great bottles from all over France (highly unusual in this part of the world), tapas-style tasting plates at the wine bar, a sculpture garden with the possibility of picnics, and a gourmet restaurant.

Throughout July and August, this is also the site of weekly open-air film screenings (or films in their screening room if it rains). *Route Verdon, D1 Rond Point des Vendangeurs, 33460 Arsac. Tel: 05 56 39 04 90. www.la-winery.com. Free admission.*

station is an easy walk from the town centre. The many châteaux can be reached on foot from the tourist office

Bridge over the Dordogne at Libourne

Vineyard of Château Canon, Saint-Émilion

(*place des Créneaux*), and there is a small train that loops around the vines, making this one of the best destinations for non-drivers.

La Librairie des Colporteurs
Hiding down a tiny side street at the bottom end of the village (head to the place du Marché and wind your way outwards from there), this charming bookshop manages to give the impression of having been here for centuries even though it is really fairly recent. Inside, there is a mix of antique and second-hand books in both English and French, and you are free to browse for as long as you want, often accompanied by soft music and the offer of a freshly brewed cup of coffee.
5 rue de Thau. Tel: 05 57 24 29 61. Email: info@antiquebook.info. www.librairie-des-colporteurs.com. Open: daily 11am–6.30pm. Free admission.

Macaroons
You can't visit Saint-Émilion without sampling the local specialities. Made from an 18th-century recipe, they are a delicious mixture of egg whites, sugar and crushed almonds. The most
(*Cont. on p44*)

The Médoc islands and lakes

It's easy to concentrate solely on wine when you venture up into the Médoc, but that would be ignoring the large tracts of the land that are not covered in vines. Besides wide-open areas of rural spaces for hiking and grazing cattle, known as the Médoc Vert (Green Médoc), and some attractive coastal towns once you reach the Atlantic edge of the peninsula (*see 'The Atlantic Coast', pp52–65*), the area has some large freshwater lakes and even a few islands in the Garonne river.

The lakes are set inland from the coast, but all fall on the eastern side of the peninsula, starting with Lacanau just above the Bassin d'Arcachon. The further north you head, the wilder and more dramatic the scenery becomes and the more unspoilt the lakes. Lacanau lake is lined with pine trees, covers an area of almost 1,420 hectares (3,500 acres) and has some lovely beaches. There are places to hire boats so you can sail around and investigate the coves and hidden bays, as well as walking and cycling trails around the outside of the lake.

If you travel further up to Carcan-Hourtin lakes (together they form one of the largest natural freshwater lakes

in France), things get quieter and more family-oriented. There are excellent fishing opportunities here, and the town of Hourtin has a lovely marina where sailing boats and small pleasure craft bob alongside a dock covered with several small cafés. This is a good spot for those wishing to learn to sail, and a number of sailing schools operate from here.

The much smaller Étang de Cousseau sits between Carcan and Lacanau and is a nature reserve, often humid and hot from the effect of being so close to the ocean and the two larger lakes. It's a haven for birds, butterflies, toads and all manner of wildlife making its home among the moss, marshland, water and wild-flower pastureland. A 3km (nearly 2-mile) walking and cycling path takes you through the different landscapes of the nature reserve, and a half-day walking circuit with explanatory signs is also provided. (You must park your car at a central parking area and then take the footpath.)

The islands, in contrast, are located on the Garonne river as it heads up to the mouth of the Atlantic Ocean, mainly clustered around the town of Pauillac. At this point, the river turns into the Gironde estuary and is so

The Gironde estuary

wide that it can accommodate several islands in the centre of it – some of which are even inhabited. No commercial boats run between them and the 'mainland' but there are tours available on small boats, often leaving (from July to September only, and usually only at weekends) from the Port de Plaisance in Pauillac. The closest island to Pauillac is the Île de Patiras. This island is around 3km (2 miles) long and sits around 2km (1¼ miles) in from either bank. There is a vineyard on the island, and tours and tastings are available. The Île de Fort Paté has the ruins of Fort Paté that once stood as sentry to the important port of Bordeaux. Other islands include the Île de Cazeau, the Île Verte and the Île du Nord, all of which are now important resting sites for migratory birds.

For information on the lakes: Lacanau tourist office. Tel: 05 56 03 21 01.
For information on the islands: Pauillac tourist office. Tel: 05 56 59 03 08. www.pauillac-Médoc.com
For other boat trips around the islands and estuary: Tel: 05 56 59 09 34. www.gensdestuaire.fr

famous place to get them is Madame Gachet on rue Guadet, next to the post office, but tiny stalls and artisan producers whip them up in every corner of the town. Be warned: they melt pretty quickly in your mouth, so stock up!

Organic vineyard tours

Not only the centre of Saint-Émilion but its surrounding landscape has been classified by UNESCO, so it makes sense that in 2010 the tourist office launched a new wine tourism circuit explaining the local biodiversity project. The worthwhile visit comprises a walk (of around 30 minutes, with a bilingual guide) to a wine estate practising organic or biodynamic winemaking, then a picnic lunch at the estate with their wines (and of course all organic produce, much of it locally produced), followed by a tour of the town itself.

Tel: 05 57 55 28 28. www.saint-emilion-tourisme.com. Open: Apr–Sept one Thur a month. Admission charge.

Castillon-la-Bataille

This sleepy town, on the banks of the Dordogne river, has a large market held every Saturday that attracts farmers, winemakers and various artisans – along with large crowds, particularly throughout the summer months. Besides the market, other attractions in the town include some beautiful medieval gates, a stone bridge across the river, and wide stone quays. This riverside location is the site of a newly opened wine store and cultural centre that belongs to UK wine merchants Direct Wines (called The Chai on the Quai, *Tel: 05 57 40 13 31*). The centre offers events and tastings through the year, but more particularly over the summer. And besides all this, one of the biggest events in the region is held here twice a week through July and August: the re-creation of the Battle of Castillon, the event that saw the English cast out of Aquitaine after 300 years in charge (*see 'Festivals and events', pp20–21*). The town only added the 'Battle' part of its name in 1953, perhaps realising the marketing and tourism value of such a move.

The Médoc

The Médoc is a narrow strip of land that edges northwards of Bordeaux city, with the Atlantic Ocean on the western side and the Garonne river on the east. A bank of pine trees offers protection from the ocean breezes, and large stones – that in some places reach almost puddingstone size as in the Rhône Valley, but are more usually fine pebbles – make this perfect vine-growing territory. Many of the biggest names in the world of wine are located up here, and the best way to explore them is by taking the D2 road – known as La Route des Châteaux – as it hugs the banks of the Garonne and meanders up through star-quality villages such as Margaux, Saint-Julien, Pauillac and Saint-Estèphe.

Château Margaux

Château d'Agassac

This small but perfectly proportioned château (complete with moat and fairy-tale towers) within striking distance of central Bordeaux offers several innovative and fun visits, including an iPod tour where children can search for a princess hiding in the château's tower. They also produce a yearly chocolate to match with the most recent wine vintage.

15 rue du Château d'Agassac.
Tel: 05 57 88 15 47. www.agassac.com.
Free admission.

Château Lanessan

This is a good visit for families, with a focus on horses (the vineyard uses some traditional horsepower for ploughing most of its vines). There is an interesting Musée de Cheval, and the chance to explore the vines in a horse and buggy – or even on horseback with an experienced guide. Various tutored wine-tasting options are also available, from tastings of old wines to understanding how the blending of different grape varieties affects the taste of the final wine.

33460 Cussac-Fort-Médoc. Tel: 05 56 58 94 80. www.lanessan.com.
Admission charge.

Château Mouton Rothschild

There is always a thrill in visiting the most prestigious châteaux in Bordeaux, but this is one of the few of the really top tier that make it relatively simple for visitors to access. The wine museum – one of the first forays into wine tourism in France when it opened back in the 1960s – is due to reopen its doors in summer 2011, and will contain an exhibition of all the original art works of the labels, painted by iconic artists such as Andy Warhol and Picasso. After the reopening, wine tasting will be treated separately and will be more strictly for professionals.

33250 Pauillac. Tel: 05 56 73 20 20.
www.dbpr.com. Train: to Pauillac train station, then taxi. Admission charge.

Graves

The area to the south of Bordeaux city is known as Graves, due to the gravelly soil that you find there. This region contains some interesting archaeological sites and Gallo-Roman remains, as well as the location of some of the earliest vines in Bordeaux, dating back over 2,000 years. More recent national treasures are also found here, such as the Château de la Brède, where the philosopher Montesquieu lived and worked. As you head further down south towards Les Landes and the Lot-et-Garonne, the landscape becomes less about vines and more about polyculture.

Bazas

This pretty cathedral town is best known for its beef, which rates as some of the best in France alongside that of Limousin and Charolais, and is so fêted that there is a festival held here in honour of Bazas cattle every February, where prize examples are led around the town and a huge celebration takes place in the main square, the Place de la Cathédrale. These huge animals produce a succulent meat that is usually served grilled over vine cuttings and seasoned with shallots in a red-wine sauce. Besides this attraction (although the butchers' shops alone can be enough to attract visitors from far and wide around), the Place de la Cathédrale itself is impressive, with a large 13th-century Gothic cathedral. A lively market is held every Saturday morning in the square and under the arcades.

Château de la Brède

Not known for its wine, this château is rather more like a stately home similar to those found in the English countryside. One of the few moated castles in the area, and extraordinarily well preserved, the château is also surrounded by English-style gardens. Expect plenty of proud displays of Montesquieu's philosophical musings, as one of Bordeaux's most famous sons.
Avenue du Château, 33650 La Brède. Tel: 05 56 20 20 49.
www.chateaulabrede.com. Open: Easter–end Sept daily. Admission charge.

Château Roquetaillade

Again, not a wine château (although they do make a few bottles), but a listed monument and a perfectly preserved medieval castle. For little ones, there's a petting zoo and farm over the road.

33210 Mazères. Tel: 05 56 76 14 16.
http://chateauroquetaillade.free.fr. Open: Jul–Aug daily 11am–5pm; rest of the year 3pm & 4pm visits. Admission charge.

Château Smith Haut Lafitte

A hotel, restaurant and wine spa, as well as a working wine estate, this château in the region of Pessac-Leognan can be reached within 25 minutes of central Bordeaux and is one of the most rewarding visits in the Bordeaux area. The estate is practising organic and increasing biodynamic farming, and there is also a barrel-maker on site, giving you the chance to see this ancient tradition in action.
33650 Martillac. Tel: 05 57 83 11 22.
www.smith-haut-lafitte.com. Open: daily. Admission charge.

Sauternes

The village of Sauternes has an attractive church that has been smartly restored, a lovely view over surrounding vines, and a good number of excellent restaurants, cafés and wine shops. There are also several properties within walking distance of the church where they will explain to you in detail the painstaking work that goes into making the famous sweet wine that comes from this part of Bordeaux. The Maison du Sauternes holds regular tastings.
Maison du Sauternes, 14 place de la Mairie. Tel: 05 56 76 69 83.
www.maisondusauternes.com. Free admission.

Bordeaux and vineyards

Drive: Entre-deux-Mers and the Côtes

This picturesque drive takes you high above the Gironde estuary and through numerous attractive villages, past cliff dwellings and old fishermen's huts, to a fortress and a beautiful nature reserve.

Allow a day to cover the 170km (100 miles). This can also be split into two drives: one for Entre-deux-Mers and one for Bourg and Blaye.

From central Bordeaux, take the D10 south for 30km (19 miles) in the direction of Cadillac.

1 Cadillac

A smart market town with an arcaded central square, Cadillac also has a large 17th-century castle, Château des Ducs d'Épernon, which has a good exhibition of tapestries and painted ceilings.

Silhouette of the Blaye citadel

Take the Avenue de la Libération out of town towards the village of Mouleyre, then the D13 through the village of Capian and on to Créon. The drive is 19km (12 miles) altogether.

2 Créon and the Abbaye de la Sauve-Majeure

Créon is a well-preserved bastide town with two weekly markets on Wednesday and Saturday. Take a short detour down to the village of La Sauve, just 3km (2 miles) south on the D671, and explore the Abbaye de la Sauve-Majeure, partly in ruins but still with a tower that you can climb up for far-reaching views of the area.

Head back to Créon and take the D20 in the direction of Libourne. 5km (3 miles) from Créon, you'll reach Saint-Germain-du-Puch.

3 Saint-Germain-du-Puch

Make a quick stop in this pretty Entre-deux-Mers village. There is an excellent restaurant here,

L'Atmosphère, that makes for a good lunch stop.

Continue for 5km (3 miles) along the D1089e into Libourne, then pass around the town taking the D670 through Fronsac, La Rivière and Cadillac-en-Fronsadais, always following signs for Bourg. In total, this part of the road covers around 40km (25 miles).

4 Bourg

This beautiful fortified village, built on a rocky outcrop and looking down onto the Gironde estuary, still has many of its medieval walls intact. Look out for the local speciality of caramelised figs, known as *figues de Bourg*.

Take the Route de la Corniche for the 12km (7½ miles) from Bourg to Blaye – the D669.

5 La Citadelle de Blaye

Explore this fortified citadel constructed between 1685 and 1689 by Maréchal Vauban (the region also has ruins of two others: Fort Paté and Fort Médoc).

33390 Blaye. Tel: 05 57 42 86 64.
Take the rue de la Citadelle northwards out of Blaye for 13km (8 miles) to the town of St-Ciers-sur-Gironde.

6 La Nouvelle Possession

This 97-hectare (240-acre) nature reserve makes a wonderful spot for walking or cycling. There are even horse-carriage rides throughout the summer, with binoculars provided for keen birdwatchers.

Saint-Ciers-sur-Gironde, Port des Callonges, Route D23, 33390 Blaye. Tel: 05 57 42 61 99.

At this point you are close to the border with the Charente region, where the city of Cognac is located. This is a good opportunity to head over the border to visit various cognac houses. If you are returning to Bordeaux, take the D18, then the D254 to join the A10 motorway for 65km (40 miles) back to central Bordeaux.

Wines of southwest France

Southwest France contains some of the world's most celebrated wines, and also some of its least known. The vineyards of the Médoc, Pomerol and Saint-Émilion contain names such as Château Margaux, Château Ausone and Pétrus – each one with bottles selling for hundreds of pounds and made from the internationally renowned grape varieties of Cabernet Sauvignon and Merlot. Other corners of the region offer little-known wines that can be discovered for just a few euros a bottle and are crafted from indigenous grape varieties – such as Négrette or Odenc – that are barely known even a few kilometres down the road.

Overall, besides the 54 appellations of Bordeaux, southwest France has 18 appellations and 19 *vins de pays* (also known as IGT following recent EU changes) and is a treasure trove for all styles of wines. Add to this the sheer number of different styles, the fact that many are not exported, and the fact that many are made by winemakers who are working family plots that have been handed down over the centuries, and you really start to feel the heart and soul that goes into these bottles – and you realise what a great opportunity a holiday in

this region is, as you discover wines that you would never get to experience back at home.

The best way to get to know these wines is to get into a car – with plenty of boot space – and start heading for cellars. Gaillac, Marcillac and Irouléguy, for example, are regions that are dotted with vines, full of gorgeous scenery and welcoming villages. They produce wines that offer the rich taste of the southwest but are rarely seen outside of the immediate region. The three best-known red wine regions, besides Bordeaux, are perhaps Bergerac, Cahors and Madiran, and here you'll find dozens of welcoming properties, as well as regular wine festivals throughout the year. For white-wine lovers, the Côtes de Gascogne is France's largest producer of white *vins de pays* and makes a wine that is light, crisp and supremely drinkable. The most luxurious sweet whites come from Sauternes in the Bordelais, and Jurançon, not far from Toulouse. Both of these wines make wonderful accompaniments to a country pâté, or as a rich contrast to a fruit dessert.

And once the wine tasting is done, there are many other styles of drink on offer. Where pastis reigns supreme

Traditional methods are still used for vine-ploughing

in the southeast of France, over here you're more likely to be offered a fruit liqueur (try the pear brandy from Domaine Brana in Irouléguy) or an Armagnac from one of the many producers around Condom and its Gascon neighbours. Then there's the only remaining artisan cider mill on the French side of the Pyrénées, located at Txopinondo just outside Saint-Jean-de-Luz, where you can fill your glass direct from the cask. This traditionally still, cloudy cider uses local apples that are quite distinct from those found up in Normandy, and it has no added gas or artificial sweeteners. Basque cider houses are known as *sagardotegi* and often serve the cider direct from large wooden barrels. Apples are collected from the end of September until the middle of November using the *kizkia*, a tool that resembles a stick with a nail in it. The apples are crushed just as grapes are for wine, and put into the traditional *sagardotegi* vat, where the juice undergoes fermentation and is then stored in barrels (usually oak or chestnut) to mature over three or four months.

For more information, visit *www.oenoland-aquitaine.com*

The Atlantic Coast

The Côte d'Argent, or Silver Coast, follows the Atlantic Ocean down the entire west side of France, from Normandy and Brittany in the north right down to Spain. Here in southwest France, it traces for over 250km (155 miles) from the mouth of the Garonne estuary in the Gironde, known as La Pointe de Grave, down past the chic coastal resorts of Arcachon and Pyla.

Then it continues onwards to the south past the surfers' haunts of Mimizan and Capbreton, and winds slowly down towards the Spanish border, where Biarritz and Saint-Jean-de-Luz offer spa resorts, serious waves and excellent foodie opportunities.

The Garonne estuary

The coast contains the longest single stretch of beach in France, and for large parts offers many kilometres of uninterrupted walking, horse riding, kite-surfing and swimming. If driving down the coastal road, however, be aware that although very pretty, the road itself is set a little back from the coast because of the dunes and pine trees that edge the ocean, and because of concerns over erosion. To get the wonderful sea views, you will have to drive into the beach resorts themselves.

THE GIRONDE COAST
La Pointe du Médoc

The first stretch of the southwest Côte d'Argent really begins here, in Le Verdon-sur-Mer at the tip of the Médoc peninsula, and drops downwards along a stretch of coast that is fairly wild, especially at first. At this point, you have good access to the vineyards of the Médoc, and it is easy to enjoy a holiday that combines surfing, sailing and wine tasting. There is a large port here,

known as the Port du Médoc, with some moorings for pleasure boats (and they are trying to encourage this side of their activity), but it remains largely a business port.
Le Verdon-sur-Mer. Tel: 05 56 09 69 75. www.port-medoc.com

Le Phare de Cordouan (Cordouan Lighthouse)

The large, still-working Cordouan Lighthouse is one of the few lighthouses that continue to be operated by a lighthouse keeper. Located around 7km (4¼ miles) off the coast and rising 67m (220ft), the tower has been fully restored in recent years, and boat trips take visitors throughout the summer from both Royan and Le Verdon-sur-Mer. There is a small jetty for disembarking from the boat and walking up to the lighthouse, and it is also possible to climb the 311 steps to the top, passing on your way a chapel within the lighthouse itself.
Le Verdon-sur-Mer. Tel: 05 56 09 61 78. www.pharedecordouan.com

Soulac-sur-Mer

An artist retreat at the very tip of the Gironde estuary, Soulac-sur-Mer is an old-fashioned coastal resort that has a good stretch of beach with surfing and sailing schools, but is also close to forest that offers walking, cycling and horse riding. The town really sets itself apart, however, by concentrating also on its cultural offerings. The 12th-century Romanesque basilica, Notre-Dame-de-

la-Fin-des-Terres, is a UNESCO World Heritage Site, there is a good museum of art and archaeology, and there are 500 'neocolonial-style' villas in the *Village Ancien* (Old Village). Soulac also hosts a yearly festival where a classic steam train runs from Bordeaux city up to the town, which returns to how it was at the end of the 19th century.

Moulin de Vensac

This 18th-century windmill (although moved to its current site in the mid-19th century) still grinds grain into flour today and is one of the very few in France. It stands as a reminder of the time when the Médoc, with its incredibly flat landscape (the highest point being 45m/148ft above sea level), was filled with such windmills. The half-hour visit shows you the workings of the mill and explains its history, and you can also buy flour.

19 route du Moulin, 33590 Vensac. Tel: 05 56 09 45 00. www.moulindevensac.fr. Open: Jul–Aug daily 10am–12.30pm & 2.30–6.30pm; Jun & Sept weekends 10.30am–12.30pm & 2.30–6.30pm; Apr, May & Oct Sun 2.30–4.30pm. Admission charge.

Lacanau beach

Right next to the Lac de Lacanau (*see p42*), things get distinctly younger in feel once you hit the beach. This is surfing and skateboarding territory, and the young crowd don't seem to notice that most of the facilities could do with a good spruce-up.

Bassin d'Arcachon

The three resorts of Arcachon, Pyla and Cap Ferret in this bay make up the low-key summer destination of many Parisians and well-heeled Bordelais. Oyster beds are dotted throughout the Bassin d'Arcachon, the large bay that loops leisurely around for 100km (62 miles) of coastline, with the town of Arcachon at one tip and Cap Ferret peninsula at the other. Big enough to be seen as an inland sea, with tides and sandy beaches, the bay offers safe swimming and boating opportunities, as well as countless gourmet pleasures. Among the celebrity fans of Cap Ferret are Philippe Starck, Audrey Tautou, and numerous French media stars. French singer Pascal Obispo even wrote a song, 'L'île aux oiseaux', about the area. You

---

OYSTER FARMERS

In total, there are 400 farmers across the whole 15,500 hectares (38,300 acres) of the bay, working over 786 hectares (1,940 acres) of oyster parks that produce 12,000 tonnes each year. It's not the biggest oyster region in France (that would be the Charente-Maritime), but 70 per cent of the 4 million baby oysters needed to keep all the oyster regions of France stocked up each year are born in the warm waters of Arcachon's bay. A select few farms – such as **Catherine Roux** in Cap Ferret and **Cabanne 118** in Gujan-Mestras – allow you to accompany the farmers as they head out to the beds.

Cabanne 118, Port de la Barbotière, Digue Est, 33470 Gujan-Mestras. Tel: 06 84 98 06 84. Roux, Quartiers des Pêcheurs du Cap Ferret. Tel: 05 56 60 67 97.

Dawn over the Arcachon oyster beds

might not recognise the celebrities though: once you get to the Bassin, barefoot chic is what it's all about. The Porsches and Audis are hidden away, the Mini Moke is brought out of the garage (rumour has it that one household had their Jeep specially muddied by their interior designer to blend in), and life returns to the simple pleasures of discussing what fish has been caught that morning and how best to cook it that night.

Dune de Pyla

Europe's tallest sand dune is 105m (345ft) tall, 500m (1,640ft) wide and over 2.7km (1¾ miles) in length. In total, it contains over 60 million cubic metres of sand! It's not easy to climb to the top (although there are steps built into the side for the upwards trajectory if you leave from the main car park at Pyla), but the views are amazing, looking out over the Banc d'Arguin sandbank, the Cap Ferret peninsula,

the oyster beds, and the Atlantic Ocean beyond.
www.dune-pyla.com. Open: main entrance dawn–dusk. Train: station at La-Teste-du-Buch is 30km (19 miles) away.

Le Phare du Cap Ferret (Cap Ferret Lighthouse)

Reaching over 53m (174ft) high, this still-working lighthouse has a small exhibition room downstairs with a film narrated by the son of a former lighthouse keeper. There are 258 steps to the top, with views over the entire Bassin d'Arcachon and the many oyster beds to reward you for your efforts.

33970 Lège-Cap-Ferret. Tel: 05 56 03 94 49. Open: daily 10am–7pm. Closed: mid-Nov to mid-Dec. Train to Arcachon, then boat over to Cap Ferret. Admission charge.

Parc Mauresque

In the Ville d'Hiver in Arcachon, the gardens of the Parc Mauresque are worth a visit. Climb up to the Sainte-Cécile observation platform (built by Gustav Eiffel, who seems to have been France's most hardworking architect) for an amazing view over Arcachon and its bay.

33120 Arcachon. Free admission. Train from Bordeaux Saint-Jean to Arcachon.

The enormous Dune de Pyla

Cap Ferret Lighthouse

Parc Ornithologique du Teich (Le Teich Bird Park)

Among the largest bird sanctuaries in France, the park hosts over 260 species of migratory birds and around 80 permanently resident birds. Discover the park either through self-guided walking circuits (up to 6km/3¾ miles in length, although there are several shorter ones also), or by guided tour. There are viewing stations with binocular spots throughout the park, and a brasserie and boutique on site. From here you can also easily access the Leyre Delta, open for exploration by canoe, small boat or sea canoe.
Maison de la Nature du Bassin d'Arcachon. Tel: 05 56 22 80 93.
www.parc-ornithologique-du-teich.com.
Open: daily 10am–dusk. Admission

charge. Train from Bordeaux Saint-Jean to Le Teich, then a 15-minute walk from the station.

Villa Algérienne (The Algerian Villa)

Only the chapel remains of this villa, but it is one of the oddities of the area, and quite possibly the only Catholic chapel in the world built in a Moorish style. It was originally constructed by Léon Lesca, a civil engineer who built the modern port of Algiers in the mid-19th century. Back in France, he purchased an estate on the Cap Ferret peninsula and built his Moorish villa.
33970 L'Herbe. Free admission.

The Atlantic Coast

PROTECTING THE COASTLINE

The Aquitaine coastline has been a protected national treasure since the 1970s. But pollution from increased tourism and diesel boat traffic, plus climate change resulting in increasingly violent storms and a rise in rainfall, has seen a dramatic speeding up of erosion along the coastline. Cliffs are crumbling into the sea, and the dunes that protect many coastal communities are in danger. Discussions as to how to solve the problem are ongoing. In Arcachon's bay, all owners of beachside property must join an association called SIBA which manages and protects the bay, mainly by redistributing sand to guard against erosion. Further down the coast, Capbreton has a €4.5 million hydraulic system that sucks up sand from a beach 1km (²/₃ mile) to the north, and sends it south, spraying triple the amount of sand that was previously moved by trucks. The Pays Basque, with its more dramatically craggy coastline, inserts stabilisers into the cliffs to drain the water.

Surfing southwest France

If you are a true surfing enthusiast, the Côte d'Azur is going to hold little attraction, because the waves there are virtually non-existent. There is surfing up on the Brittany coastline and around La Rochelle up to the north, but few places equal the Aquitaine coastline for regularity of swells and the high likelihood of good weather to accompany them.

But you don't need to be out at sea to surf in this part of France – even the rivers allow surfers to get out their boards when the Mascaret wave travels down the Garonne and Dordogne rivers. This natural phenomenon (arising because they are tidal rivers, and this wave is a tidal bore) sees waves that can reach up to 2m (6½ft) high, allowing surfers to ride them for up to 15 or 20 minutes at a time. There are only a few spots in the world where these tidal bores exist, and the Bordeaux region is one of them. And one of the best places to catch this unusual wave is Saint-Pardon in Vayres, where an annual Fête du Mascaret is held in September. Waves occur year-round, but usually the best are during the high tides of August and September, and they are generally most

impressive where the river is at its most shallow, thus allowing the wave to reach its full height. A good website for following the progress of the waves and ensuring you don't miss the best dates is *http://mascaretgironde.free.fr*

Back on the Atlantic Ocean, it's the serious surfers who colonise the waves, and the potential for big surf attracts enthusiasts from all over the world. The summer months especially attract large numbers of professional and amateur surfers, and there are competitions held at pretty much every spot along the coast. Some of the best competitions to attend are the O'Neill Night Surf and the Vans

KEY SURFING EVENTS IN THE SOUTHWEST

Sooruz Lacanau Pro. Held in August each year, this is one of the qualifying stages for the World Championships of Surfing and Long Board. Expect plenty of events to keep spectators happy alongside the true competitors.
Office de Tourisme, Lacanau. Tel: 05 56 03 21 01. www.lacanau.com
Stand Up Paddle Surf World Tour. Held in May every year, this brings together the world's best Paddle Surfers, a traditional sport practised in Hawaii that is catching on in the wider surfing world.
Plage de la Chambre d'Amour, Anglet.

Royal Single Trophy – seen as the Woodstock of surfing events because of its retro 1970s feel. Both of these events are held in the low-key resort of Anglet, close to Biarritz, and have evolved into large festivals with music and entertainment along the beach. A useful website for finding out about upcoming surf events is *www.zelittoralattitude.fr*

But you don't need to be an expert, or even a talented amateur, to try out the magic of surfing the Atlantic waves. A good place to get started is with an approved surf school, where courses can be adapted for all ages and levels of bravery and incompetence. Do remember that even on the hottest days, this is still the Atlantic Ocean, so it's a brave soul who surfs without a full wetsuit. For all levels of courses, try the Biarritz Association of Surf Clubs for some good addresses to get you started (*www.surfingbiarritz.com*).

Big surf near Biarritz

MIMIZAN TO CAPBRETON

You are right in the heart of the Côte d'Argent here, with buzzy coastal resorts that attract a young crowd over the summer months.

Mimizan

A lively crowd heads to this breezy summer resort. There is a casino and several good golf courses, hotels and restaurants here, reflecting its status as a fully fledged tourist resort. There are, however, plenty of quiet spots, with access to cycling and walking routes into the Landes forest and lakes. Mimizan was the spot of the first transatlantic flight from France to New York in 1929, and a statue of airplane wings stands at the entrance to the Plage des Ailes (Mimizan North Beach).

Le Musée de Mimizan–Prieuré (Mimizan Priory Museum)

A UNESCO World Heritage monument, the bell tower, with its chancel and nave, is the only remaining relic of this priory, which was one of the largest in southwest France in the Middle Ages.

9 rue de l'Abbaye, 40200 Mimizan.
Tel: 05 58 09 00 61. Email:
musee@mimizan.com.
Open: office mid-Jun to mid-Sept Mon–Sat 9am–6pm; rest of the year Mon–Fri; Jul–Aug Wed until 10pm.
Always call ahead to arrange a guided visit. Admission charge. Train to Mimizan station.

Contis-Plage

Just a few kilometres down the road from the busier resort of Mimizan, this cheerful seaside town consists of little more than one main road lined with shops, restaurants and ice-cream parlours. The town also has an active cinema, with a large number of arts films shown, often in English, especially during the International Festival of Contis, held in September each year.

Le Phare du Contis-Plage (Contis-Plage Lighthouse)

The only lighthouse in Les Landes, this has 183 steps, with gorgeous views at the top to reward your efforts. It's strikingly black and white, in contrast to the ones at Cap Ferret and Capbreton. Every Thursday in July and August a demonstration of resin tapping is given by a former artisan in this trade, which used to be one of the key economic activities in Les Landes.

rue du Phare, 40170 Contis-Plage.
Tel: 05 58 51 30 92.
www.contis-tourisme.com.
Admission charge.

Moliets et Maa and Hossegor

At Moliets et Maa, there is easy access to La Réserve Naturelle du Courant d'Huchet (*see 'Lac du Léon', pp125–6*), where you can take sea canoes down remote and beautiful stretches of river. Hossegor puts the emphasis a little more firmly on the water, with its huge swathes of beach, a canal and a saltwater lake. The town itself is very elegant, with traditional Landaise houses, and a seafront that is a classified architectural site.

Capbreton

The highly attractive port here is where the two towns of Capbreton and Hossegor meet. Capbreton is significantly larger than Hossegor, and is a big sporting centre, offering everything from fishing to windsurfing, golf to sunbathing.

Quai Pompidou, Port Capbreton. Tel: 05 58 72 21 23.

Écomusée de la Pêche

This attractive museum provides a window into one of the major employers of the region – the fishing industry. Placed in the context of sustainability and tradition, it also has an aquarium of local species, and offers a wider look at ocean activities, from scuba diving to surfing.

Maison du Port, avenue Georges Pompidou, 40130 Capbreton. Tel: 05 58 72 40 50. Email: contact@ecopeche.fr. www.ecopeche.fr. Open: Apr–Sept daily; Oct–Mar Wed, Sat & Sun. Admission charge.

The Atlantic Coast

Mimizan

BIARRITZ AND SAINT-JEAN-DE-LUZ

The coastal towns of Biarritz and Saint-Jean-de-Luz are neighbours, but they couldn't be more different. The latter is slightly closer to the Spanish border and is still an active fishing port, with anchovies, tuna and sardines being the main catches, while its neighbour is a laid-back surfing hangout with excellent shopping opportunities. But what they definitely have in common is gourmet potential. Fish is of course the most important thing on local menus in both ports, and there are plenty of seafront restaurants to enjoy. A large fish market is held on Tuesdays, Fridays and Saturdays in Saint-Jean-de-Luz,

and daily in the Halles de Biarritz. There is also a tuna festival held every July in Saint-Jean-de-Luz. Biarritz has its own festival in June, celebrating the Spanish influence on its foods and culture, while numerous shops and restaurants in both towns also celebrate the best produce of the wider Basque region year-round. This is a great way to find take-home goodies, so make sure you give at least a couple of hours over to browsing the shops.

Biarritz

Biarritz is international in feel, with a young and laid-back vibe. Its large beaches and seaside walkways are given over to surfers and joggers. It was once

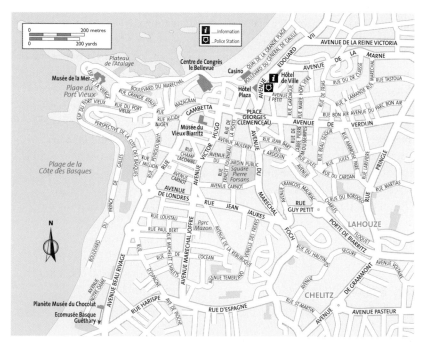

one of the most important ports in France, and its faded 1930s glamour makes it a wonderful place for a gentle weekend (although less gentle in April, when the annual surfing competition is held). The essential walk in Biarritz is on the promenade along the Grande Plage, past the Casino Barrière with its Art Deco curves and up towards the craggy promontory with its Musée de la Mer.

Musée de la Mer

Don't expect a cutting-edge aquarium – rather, this is strictly old-school in style, with an emphasis on local species and exhibits looking at conservation projects around the seas of the southwest. There are a few more exotic species, from sharks to seals (with a daily feeding display), but the real attraction is the gentle pace of the exhibitions, and the aquarium's location directly opposite the Rocher de Vierge, a statue of the Virgin Mary that was erected to keep local fishermen safe from harm. The statue stands high above the rocks on a promontory, and is accessible via a viewing platform from which you can see the whole Basque coast stretching away.
Plateau de l'Atalaye. Tel: 05 59 22 33 34. www.museedelamer.com. Open: daily 9.30am–12.30pm & 2–6pm. Closed: Nov–Mar Mondays. Admission charge.

Planète Musée du Chocolat (Chocolate Museum)

Sweet-toothed visitors (and anyone with children) shouldn't miss this small

The Rocher de Vierge, Biarritz

but perfectly formed museum. The visit starts off with a film about the history of chocolate production in the area, and has several exhibitions devoted to chocolate sculptures and vintage advertising and packaging, as well as looking at tools and traditions for making chocolate all over the world. There's even the chance for chocolate sampling, plus a cup of hot chocolate at the end of the visit – and good luck getting out of the boutique without a serious dent in your holiday budget.
14 avenue du Beau Rivage. Tel: 05 59 23 27 72. www.planetemuseeduchocolat.com. Open: school term Mon–Sat 10am–12.30pm & 2.30–6.30pm; school holidays daily 10am–6.30pm. Admission charge.

Biarritz Casino

Guéthary

This small village, popular with artists and foodies, is located directly in between Biarritz and Saint-Jean-de-Luz, and is a great base for holidays. It has a lively port and plenty of green spaces and quiet streets, as well as two Michelin-starred restaurants (*see 'Directory', p178*). The best way to explore is on foot, as the town centre is compact and walking routes are indicated. The best (low-key, not Michelin-starred) restaurants are located on the beachfront or on the craggy coves a little out of the town centre, but don't miss the town hall with its traditional Basque low-rise form, or the Saint Nicolas church, which is a great example of a Basque church with tiered wooden balconies. There is also the classic fronton (a kind

of half wall) for the traditional regional game of pelota. This is a type of palm-ball game, played either with bare hands or a wooden racket, that is popular all over the Basque region. If you manage to visit in the early evening, you'll find half the town hanging out around here.
Tourist office, 74 rue du Comte de Swiecinski. Tel: 05 59 26 56 60. www.guethary-france.com. Local train from Biarritz or Saint-Jean-de-Luz train stations.

Saint-Jean-de-Luz

This beautiful town, practically nudging the Spanish border, has developed in recent years into an upmarket, chic coastal retreat, with wonderful restaurants where you can indulge in the gastronomic pleasures of the region – you are really in Basque country here, and the fabulous flavours infuse everything. A stroll through Saint-Jean-de-Luz will not disappoint (*see pp66–7*).

Écomusée Basque

On the road into Saint-Jean-de-Luz from Biarritz, this makes a great short stop. The attractively laid-out museum has a re-creation of a traditional Basque village and explains various local crafts and traditions in a tasteful and enjoyable way. There is also an excellent restaurant (try one of their tapas plates of Brebis and local hams, especially good eaten outside in the garden) and an excellent boutique that stocks local interior products – from towels to plates to linen – made by Jean Vier, whose eye for interior design has meant his products are now sold in Paris, London and New York.

64500 Saint-Jean-de-Luz. Tel: 05 59 51 06 06. Open: Jul–Aug daily 10am–6.30pm; Apr–Jun 10–11.15am & 2.30–5.30pm. Admission charge (admission to boutique is free).

Jardin Botanique

This beautiful garden has a stunning view over the bay from its location on the Archilua cliffs. Just 2.5 hectares (4 acres) in size, the sound of the waves fills its quiet spaces, and it has an excellent range of trees, flowers and plants from around the world. A research and conservation centre holds regular exhibitions and lectures.
31 avenue Gaetan Bernoville. www.jardinbotaniquelittoral-saintjeandeluz.org. Open: May–Sept Wed, Sat & Sun 11am–6pm; Mar–Apr 11am–5pm; rest of the year 2–5pm. Admission charge.

Saint-Jean-de-Luz

Walk: Saint-Jean-de-Luz

The beautiful coastal resort of Saint-Jean-de-Luz is set in a stunning natural harbour, with the city arching in a compact and orderly manner around the curve of the bay and spreading out from a central marina. It makes for a lovely place to walk around.

The whole 4km (2½-mile) walk will take around three hours, or longer if you don't take the short cuts offered by the navette boats!

Start at Digue de Socoa at the southern edge of the bay.

1 The lighthouse

While you're feeling energetic at the start of the walk, climb to the top of the lighthouse to get stunning views of the town of Saint-Jean-de-Luz (although technically at this point you are in the neighbouring town of Ciboure). If that feels too much, just a stroll out to the far end of the Digue de Socoa also gives a good feel of just how sweepingly perfect this bay is. There is also a fishing port here – smaller than the central port, but often busy with fishermen hauling their catch back on shore, and great for watching this ritual.
Either take the navette boat to the central port, or walk along the Boulevard Pierre Benoît past the Vierge de Musida and on to the Quai Maurice Ravel.

2 The port and marina

At this point, you have reached the busy central port, highly picturesque and packed with cafés, restaurants and cultural corners. Walk down rue des Coles to the 17th-century Couvent et Cloître des Récollets (Récollet Convent and Cloisters).
Cross the Pont Charles de Gaulle into Saint-Jean-de-Luz proper, then continue around the port to the Quai de l'Infante.

3 La Maison de l'Infante (The Infanta's House)

A quick step inside these well-preserved rooms gives an idea of how the town was in the mid-17th century, when the Spanish Infanta Marie-Thérèse lived here. The house was built by a wealthy merchant, who could watch the arrival and departure of his merchant ships from the first-floor windows. The current owners often hold contemporary art exhibitions here also.
Take rue Mazarin and then rue Gambetta, heading away from the main streets into the heart of the Old Town.

4 Église Saint-Jean-Baptiste

Hidden among the streets of the pedestrianised Old Town, on the place du Maréchal Foch, the rather simple façade hides an intricate interior in the largest church in the Basque region.

From here, turn down rue Gambetta, enjoying the small boutiques you pass, then cross boulevard Thiers and follow the small rue Agent Fautous to the park.

5 Parc Ducontenia

A pretty green space, where you can enjoy the Théâtre de la Nature, or allow children some fun in the playground.

Retrace your steps to boulevard Thiers, and follow it up past the elegant Grand Hôtel (stop in for some thalassotherapy if you feel ready for a pampering) to where you will rejoin the waterfront.

6 Digue de Sainte-Barbe

Along with the lighthouse, this offers one of the most impressive panoramas of Saint-Jean-de-Luz seafront and bay, this time with the added bonus of seeing the mountains rise away in the distance. From the Pointe de Sainte-Barbe, a map explains the points of interest you can see in front of you.

Follow the promenade des Rochers to the Digue aux Chevaux, and take the navette boat back to your starting place by the lighthouse. If you would rather walk, simply follow the promenade around the entire half-crescent of the bay.

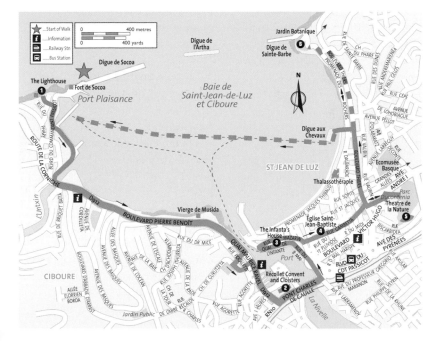

The Basque language and traditions

You'll start seeing road signs in both Basque and French as soon as you get close to the area of Bayonne, Biarritz and Saint-Jean-de-Luz, and with increasing frequency as you head up into the mountains. The Basque language seems to have no known living links to other languages (although some suggest Welsh is the closest), and is spoken by around 550,000 people in the Spanish Pyrénées, but only around 70,000 here in the French Pyrénées. It is thought that the Basque people have lived in this region for over 20,000 years. Whatever the case, their culture and language are firmly embedded in the towns and villages of the area.

The language has an official status within Spain, but not in France. However, even here its influence is still widely seen and felt, in place names, in family names, even in the attractively stylised lettering that is seen all over this part of France. This lettering has its origins in stone carving, which explains why most words tend to be written in upper case and why the letters themselves tend to be wide and strong. All of this makes the attractive 'Basque script' a memorable feature of any visit

through the Basque region, and you will see it reproduced on packaging, postcards, hotel signs and place names. You might also see the term 'Euskal Herria' (which means 'Basque Country') on addresses, and you should listen out for local inhabitants referring to themselves as *euskaldunak*.

Besides noticing the language, you will also see the Basque flag flying – most usually alongside the French *drapeau tricolore* to avoid any political incorrectness – outside the town halls of most villages. The Basque flag is similar in design to the Union Jack from the United Kingdom, but the red, white and blue have become red, green and white: red for Basque, green for hope and white for faith.

Even if the Basque language is not widely spoken today (it is important to remember that schoolchildren in this region must always speak French as their first and only official language), what is certain is that Basque traditions are still alive and well. Expect to see a form of Basque dancing at any festivals you attend, called Basque ballet, where the dancers (male and female) wear laced-on slippers and spend much of the dance showing off this footwear by twirling and kicking their feet around. The white and red colours that you see in the architecture also extend to the traditional Basque costumes that are worn at many festivals, often white trousers worn with a red cummerbund and red beret for the men, or a red skirt, white shirt and black waistcoat for the women.

Competitive sport is also a big deal. Each town or village will have its fronton – a single high wall with lines marked on it – for the Basque game of pelota (*see 'Guéthary', p64*). These walls are also often the focus of social life for the villages, with teenagers practising tennis strokes against them, or just hanging out. The Musée Basque (Basque Museum) in Bayonne (*see p73*) has a good exhibition on the sport and its accompanying culture. Other sporting activities you might see include horse racing, weight lifting, log-chopping and even tug-of-war, which usually turns into a communal event involving the whole village. The people here are very friendly – and you will be welcomed in most warmly if you decide to pick up the rope…

The Basque *ikurriña*

The French Pyrénées

The Pyrénées extend for over 400km (250 miles) from the Atlantic Ocean to the Mediterranean Sea, dipping between Navarra and Catalonia in Spain and in France through the Pays Basque, then upwards to the Béarn department, to the regional capital of Pau and the ancient port city of Bayonne. This is one of the most distinct and rewarding areas of southwest France to visit.

Here you can effortlessly slip from wild mountain spaces to bustling villages to smart market towns, and in each place the traditions of the region are to be seen fully alive and well. Up in the hills, whether walking, cycling or driving, you can expect to find mountain goats wandering along the side of the road, woolly sheep grazing along steep verges, and wild brown bears chasing fish in the mountain streams.

Among the many delicacies of the region are freshly caught fish, carefully dried hams, charcuterie, Brébis cheese from Pyrénées mountain sheep, a tangy sheep cheese called *ardigazna*, spice-infused chocolate, dense black cherry jams, Basque cider, the almond-infused *gâteau Basque*, fruit wines and liqueurs, and the tiny spicy Espelette peppers.

PAYS BASQUE

With its own special flavours and customs, the Basque region of southwest France contains some of its most picturesque villages and its most welcoming people. Expect to eat well here too – to find the most incredible restaurants in the tiniest of villages (many nationally recognised), and to stumble at almost every turn across artisan producers who will be only too happy to offer you tastings and tours. A map showing a gourmet tour of the region is available at all tourist offices.

Saint-Jean-Pied-de-Port

Located on the River Nive, the fortified town of Saint-Jean-Pied-de-Port is known for its stunning views and its citadel surrounded by ramparts. You are just 8km (5 miles) away from the Spanish border at this point, and the town is a key stop on the Compostela pilgrim route (*see pp130–31*). The town itself is lovely, with a flower-lined stone bridge crossing the river and numerous small boutiques selling Basque produce. Farmers' markets are held every week in place de Gaulle, and over the summer nearly every day it seems another local fair is happening. This is also the region for AOC Irouléguy wines (the only vineyard area of the French Basque region), and there are several properties open for visits near the village.

Citadelle de Vauban

This imposing citadel dates from the early 17th century. It was built by Pierre de Conty, but later, during the reign of Louis XIV, reinforced by Vauban, a military strategist who seems to have been behind most fortified towns and forts around France. Over the years, the citadel has served to protect the region from Spanish soldiers, and visitors can still climb to the top of the ramparts to see just why it was so effective, providing as it does excellent views of the surrounding mountains. Just below

the fortress, you can also visit the **Musée des Évêques**. This former prison (which used to hold French Resistance forces during the Nazi occupation) is now an interesting museum detailing the Route de Compostela and the history of the pilgrimage.

41 rue de la Citadelle. Tel: 05 59 37 00 91. Open: Jul–Aug daily 10am–7pm. Admission charge.

Cave d'Irouléguy

Most grape growers in this region make wine through the large local cooperative cellar, which is open for visits and organises regular tastings of both food and wine in its attractive boutique. A festival of the local wines is held every May. This cooperative

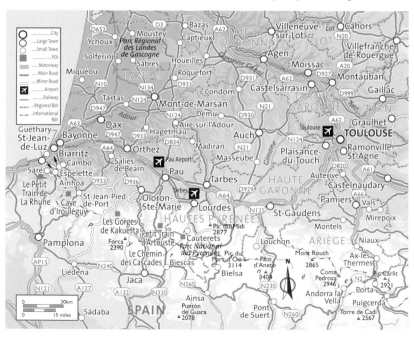

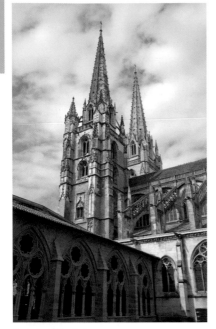

Bayonne cathedral

works with over 140 individual winemakers in the region, but the cellars and shop are in the attractive village of Saint-Étienne-de-Baïgorry, known for its arched Roman bridge over the River Nive.
Route de Saint-Jean-Pied-de-Port, 64430 Saint-Étienne-de-Baïgorry. Tel: 05 59 37 41 33. www.cave-irouleguy.com. Open: mid-Apr–Sept daily; Oct–mid-Apr Mon–Sat.

Cauterets

The centre of hiking into the national park, this peaceful village is the start of more than a dozen hiking trails and is covered in 'Getting away from it all' (*see pp134–6*).

Les Gorges de Kakuetta

This is a wild and usually deserted canyon where you can hike along footpaths to a 20m-high (66ft) waterfall and the Grotte du Lac with its stalactites and stalagmites. Not an easy walk, but absolutely worth the effort. The village of Sainte-Engrâce itself is also stunning, 630m (2,070ft) up in the mountains with a beautiful chapel.
64560 Sainte-Engrâce. Tel: 05 59 28 60 83. Open: mid-Mar–mid-Sept daily 8am–dusk. Admission charge.

Le Petit Train de La Rhune

This wonderful cog-wheeled train climbs the 825m (2,700ft) summit of La Rhune, passing wild Pottok horses along the way. The view from the top is incredible, and you can either walk back down or return by train, making it a good option if you have little ones in tow.
Col de Saint-Ignace, 64310 Sare. Tel: 08 92 39 14 25. www.rhune.com. Admission charge. Le Basque Bondissant coach service from Saint-Jean-de-Luz (Tel: 05 59 26 25 74), leaving from opposite the SCNF train station.

Bayonne

Bayonne is a few kilometres inland from Biarritz, but it is still a large port city due to its location on the River Adour, and boasts attractive wide quays and beautiful views over the Pyrénées. The Notre Dame cathedral, dramatically Gothic with beautiful cloisters, dates from the 12th century and is one of the largest in southwest France. Besides sampling the world-famous ham while you're here (*see pp16–17*), you must try some of their wonderful dark spicy chocolate flavoured with Espelette peppers.

Musée Basque (Basque Museum)
A lovely museum looking out over the Nive waterfront, this is an important centre for research and restoration of Basque art and traditions. Besides the excellent archives detailing the history of the region, there are also fascinating reconstructions of Basque villages, arts, crafts and sports.
37 quai des Corsaires. Tel: 05 59 59 08 98. www.musee-basque.com. Open: daily Tue–Sun 10am–6.30pm (Jul–Aug Wed until 10.30pm). Admission charge.

Musée d'Histoire Naturelle de Bayonne (Bayonne Natural History Museum)
Located in the middle of the Ansot nature reserve, this centre for research opened its doors to the public in June 2010 and is really worth the visit. There is a museum building, but many of the exhibits are outside in the park itself and can be explored by foot or by bike. There is also a bird sanctuary and observatory.
Plaine d'Ansot. Tel: 05 59 42 44 61. www.museum.bayonne.fr. Open: winter Tue–Sun 10.30am–6pm; summer Tue–Sun 9.30am–7.30pm. Admission charge. Electric bus from the Pont Blanc on Wed and Sat afternoons.

Le Petit Train de la Rhune

Drive: Through thc Pyrénées

A beautiful circular drive through the mountains is possible even if you are staying down on the coast and have just one day, or half a day, to spare. A good bet is to leave from Saint-Jean-de-Luz and head up into the mountains from there. You can then choose to either return the same day, or find a regional inn in which to spend the night.

In total this drive covers 133km (83 miles). If you have only half a day, stop after Espelette and return to Saint-Jean-de-Luz. Get on the D918 following signs for Ascain/Cambo-les-Bains. Take the turning for Ascain and then the D4 to Sare, 13km (8 miles) away in total.

Musée du Gâteau Basque, Sare

Make sure you go up into the centre of the village; you'll drive up a beautiful road lined with plane trees and arrive in a pretty central square. There are also some gorgeous grottoes, but the real draw here is the Gâteau Basque Museum, dedicated to all things to do with this delicious cake, and even offering visitors the chance to make their own example.

Maison Haranea, Quartier Lehenbiscay, 64310 Sare. Tel: 05 59 54 22 09. www.legateaubasque.com. Admission charge.

Head back down the plane trees road, and turn right onto the D4, then take the D306, then the stunning mountain road to Zugarramundi. This is just over the border into the Navarre region of Spain, but it is impossible to avoid criss-crossing between the two countries when exploring this area. Feel free to get out for a stroll, then continue winding down, passing through Dantxarinea back into France and the D20 into Ainhoa. In total this section is 16km (10 miles).

Ainhoa

A near-perfect Basque village (one of several in the Pays Basque to be afforded 'Most Beautiful Village in France' status), complete with gorgeous church and chapel – even the cemetery is distinctly Basque. It's worth stepping in to the Maison du Patrimoine (Heritage Museum, opposite the church) to see the large-screen film of the history of the village.

Take the D20 just 6km (3¾ miles) into Espelette.

The peppers of Espelette

Yet another heart-stoppingly charming village, famed for the tiny red peppers that, depending on the time of year, you may well see strung up outside every building in town. Also worth visiting are the Maison du Fromage (House of Cheese) and the Maison du Jambon (House of Ham), right next to each other and perfect for the dairy or meat lover in you.

Take the D918 road from Espelette and follow the River Nive along a beautiful mountain road as it climbs upwards and into Saint-Jean-Pied-de-Port. This is a slightly longer drive, at 35km (22 miles), but with rewarding scenery all along the way, and passing through the villages of Bidarray, Gahardou and Uhart-Cize.

Citadelle de Vauban

Explore the citadel and the Musée des Évêques (*see p71*), have a bite to eat at one of the cafés along the River Nive, and then wind your way back down into Biarritz.

Take the D918 to Itxassou, then the D932 until you pick up signs for the A64 motorway to take you just one exit down to Biarritz (or back to Saint-Jean-de-Luz if you are based there). This section is a further 60km (37 miles), but again you can stop along the way or spend the night in one of the villages to prolong your stay.

Typical Basque architecture, Ainhoa

Thermal spa towns of the southwest

The southwest of France is the country's leading spa region: over 900,000 people visit the thermal (meaning warm water thought to have healing properties, usually from natural spring waters) and thalassotherapy (using sea and seawater products) spas across Aquitaine each year, bringing in €45 million to the region. The Hautes- and Midi-Pyrénées continue the theme, and the whole area is peppered with resorts and simple spots for relaxation. This abundance of healing waters – proven over centuries – is due not only to the saltwater properties of the Atlantic Ocean, but also to a rich mineral water basin that covers the entire area. Some excellent bottled mineral waters also come from this part of France, the best known of which is Les Abatilles from Arcachon and Luchon in the Pyrénées.

The therapeutic values of the region's water have been recognised since Roman times, and the first recorded thermal spa in southwest France was in Dax (*see 'Les Landes', p129*), where the Romans developed the hot spring of La Nehe. Today, the town continues to be a centre for spa-seekers, with around 60,000 visitors per year (remember that in France, many of the treatments are recognised medical procedures, and are therefore covered by health insurance), and is the site of the National Institute of Thermal Therapy, the largest of its kind in Europe. Similarly, Biarritz, Eugénie-les-Bains and Saint-Jean-de-Luz remain leading spa towns, with their popularity dating from the Second Empire, when Empress Eugénie seemed to spend half the year relaxing in, and therefore popularising, the spa resorts of the southwest. (There had to be some

The Grand Café Ax-les-Thermes

Peaceful park in Louchon

benefits to being Emperor Napoleon III's wife, after all.)

Besides these large, well-recognised resorts, a few other smaller spa towns include:

Ax-les-Thermes

Offering skiing in winter and walking in summer, this resort sits at 720m (2,360ft) above sea level in the Midi-Pyrénées. The sulphurous waters here are the warmest of any Pyrenean spa town, going from 23°C (73.4°F) in La Basse to 77.8°C (172°F) in the Fontaine du Rossignol, so you can choose from a range of therapies. The town grew around the site of a leprosy hospital in the 13th century, as did the resort of Arcachon on the Atlantic Coast (see pp54–7).
www.ax-les-thermes.net

Cambo-les-Bains

One of the leading resorts in the Pays Basque region, and just 20 minutes inland from Biarritz and Saint-Jean-de-Luz, this is also the home town of Edmond Rostand, author of *Cyrano de Bergerac*. Among the many spa treatments on offer here is a week-long quit-smoking package!
www.cambolesbains.com

Louchon

Louchon has sulphurous springs and attracts plenty of – particularly elderly – visitors, who are not put off by the fairly medical atmosphere and sulphurous smells! There is an interesting vaporium, a natural underground sauna, that is worth a visit. This is also the site of an excellent bottled water.
www.thermes.louchon.fr

Salies-de-Béarn

Also known as the 'white gold town', its waters are seven times saltier than sea water, offering plenty of water therapies similar to those of the Dead Sea (which just pips it, at ten times saltier than sea water). Salt has been collected and sold from here for over 3,000 years, and exploited for its therapeutic properties since the Middle Ages. There is also a highly attractive Venice feel to the Old Town, with historic houses sitting on stilts overlooking the river, so you'll have plenty to see in between spa visits.
www.salies-de-bearn.fr

ANDORRA AND THE HAUTES-PYRÉNÉES

As you move further east towards the Pyrénées-Orientales and the Languedoc, the landscape becomes ever more dramatic. This is the best area for skiing and serious mountain climbing. This is also the side of the Pyrénées which is easily accessible from the city of Toulouse. If you like trains, cable cars and generally all things to do with heights, you are going to love it here. If not, make the most of the many mountain lakes, which you can explore and enjoy without the vertigo.

Andorra

Besides its attractions as a ski resort, this is also a lively tourist town, with only 75,000 permanent residents but ten million annual visitors, and

Caldea spa, Andorra

HOW ANDORRA GAINED INDEPENDENCE

Andorra, according to tradition, was granted a charter of independence by Charlemagne in the 9th century, as a reward for joining in his fight against the Moors. Despite various jostles ever since (it has at times been under Spanish rule, at other times French), Andorra's borders have remained unchanged since 1278. During World War II, it remained neutral and was used widely by the Resistance to get people out of France. Since 1993, it has been a parliamentary democracy (its current prime minister is Jaume Bartumeu Cassany), but it remains a tax haven, and besides tourism, the leading industry is financial services.

renowned the world over as a tax haven and duty-free port. Strictly speaking, this is not in southwest France, as Andorra is its own principality, but it is the starting point for most southwestern French ski resorts (*see pp82–3*). Head to Andorra la Vella, the capital of the principality, which lies at the meeting point of the Valira du Nord and the Valira d'Orient mountain rivers. This is where you will find the most interesting shopping opportunities, together with some attractive old stone streets and a Romanesque church. Outside of this, you are faced with wall-to-wall duty-free shops.

Pic du Midi

It's pretty difficult to top the view from here, reached by taking the cable car from La Mongie, at the foot of the Col du Tourmalet, as it ascends 1,000m

The gold crown atop the Rosary Basilica, Lourdes

(3,280ft) up to the Pic du Midi. The ride takes just 15 minutes, and once you are up there, you are standing at 2,877m (9,439ft) above sea level. As you might expect, the view on clear days is astonishing, allowing you to see over 300km (185 miles) of peaks. There is also a museum on site, an observatory (for a really amazing experience, book in for one of their Starry Night or Full Moon evenings), and a good restaurant. *rue Pierre Lamy de la Chapelle, 65200 La Mongie. Tel: 08 25 00 28 77. www.picdumidi.com.*

Open: 1 Jun–30 Sept daily 9am–4.30pm, departures every 15 minutes; rest of the year 10am–3.30pm. Admission charge (pregnant women and children under three not allowed). Train to La Mongie station.

Lourdes

Heading down slightly from the Pic du Midi, this famous spa town and religious site attracts over six million visitors each year from all over the world and has the highest concentration of hotels in France outside Paris. The people who come are here to capture some of the spirit that has reigned in the town since the Virgin Mary appeared to 14-year-old Bernadette Soubirous in 1858. The Lady appeared 18 times to the child, each time giving her instructions, asking her among other things to build a chapel at the site of the vision. There is also an 11th-century fort and an interesting Pyrenean museum. Expect it to get very crowded throughout the summer and during key religious festivals (over nine million visitors

Glasshouse in the Jardin Massey, Tarbes

made the trip in 2008 to celebrate the 150th anniversary of the Apparitions). And your sense of spirituality might just be tested when you are faced with the countless kiosks selling Lourdes postcards, Lourdes holy water, statues of the Virgin Mary (often doubling as receptacles for holy water) and wooden rosary beads.

Le Pic du Jer

This mountain (the official start of the Pyrénées according to some sources) overlooks Lourdes and is topped by a large cross which is illuminated at night. A funicular cable car (or chair-lift) takes you up to its peak (standing at 1,000m/3,280ft above sea level) in just six minutes. Once up there, you can enjoy an amazing view back over Lourdes, or stomach a slightly kitsch light-and-sound display. There is the chance to either walk or mountain bike back down along a botanic walkway.
59 avenue Francis Lagardère. Tel: 05 62 94 00 41. Email: picdujer@ville-lourdes.fr. Open: Mar–Jun & Sept–Nov daily 10am–6pm; Jul–Aug 9am–8pm. Admission charge.

Tarbes

A rather low-key resort, but very charming in parts, with a beautiful central park, Le Jardin Massey, originally landscaped by the same man who became director of the park at the palace of Versailles. The lovely museum and art gallery within the park (closed until 2011 for restoration), Le Musée

THE ORIGINAL MIRACLE OF LOURDES

The origin of Lourdes' status as a religious shrine was a young girl called Bernadette Soubirous. She was a shepherdess who came from a poor peasant family, and by all accounts was also asthmatic and generally sickly. Bernadette was 14 years old when she saw her first apparition, on 11 February 1858, of the Virgin Mary dressed in a white robe with a blue ribbon at the waist. Although most of the town didn't believe her at first, by the 15th visitation one month after the original one, 20,000 people jammed Lourdes, and soldiers were put on standby. In the same year, seven miraculous cures of the sick took place in the town. Bernadette spent the last 12 years of her life as a nun, until she died in 1879. In 1933, she was canonised as a saint by the Catholic Church.

Massey, concentrates largely on Renassiance painters.

Musée de la Déportation et de la Résistance

This fascinating museum looks at examples of resistance and fighting for freedom across the world, but concentrating largely on World War II. There are exhibits and testimonies of life in deportation camps in the Ukraine, of Resistance fighters in the Pyrénées mountains, and of the estimated 1.6 million French prisoners of war. There is also an excellent library for further research into the period.
63 rue Georges Lassalle. Tel: 05 62 51 11 60. Open: Mon–Fri 8.30am–noon & 2–5.30pm. Free admission.

Skiing in southwest France

It may not have the same glamour as skiing in the Alps, but the Pyrénées offer a wealth of opportunities for skiers and snowboarders – with the distinct advantage that there are many green and blue slopes for young children and families to learn on. Resorts here also tend to be a little less crowded and slightly better value than those on the eastern side of France. There are fewer black runs than in the Alps (this is the most difficult level of slope, for the experienced skier only), but almost all resorts have red runs, and most have one or two black ones for those who absolutely don't want to miss out. In all there are over 200 summits that climb over 2,000m (6,560ft); you have to go over to the Spanish side and Pico d'Aneto for the highest point at just over 3,400m (11,150ft). In total, the Midi-Pyrénées region is host to 38 ski resorts and 1,000km (620 miles) of marked pistes.

Think carefully about the kind of ski holiday you are looking for before booking. There are snow parks, which contain freestyle options from jumps and rails for the more daring skiers, as at resorts such as **Peyragudes** (*www.peyragudes.com*). This also has fifteen red and three black runs, and is popular with snowboarders.

The largest resort in the area is **Tourmalet/La Mongie**, right at the base of the Pic du Midi mountain. It provides 100km (62 miles) of slopes and 32km (20 miles) of lifts to choose from (*www.bagneresdebigorre-lamongie.com*), the latter rising to

Off-piste in the Pyrénées

La Pierre Saint-Martin

nearly 2,500m (8,200ft) in altitude. This resort has some good restaurants and spas, and plenty of ski schools and 'snow clubs' for little ones who are too young to ski.

Most French resorts accept young skiers from the age of three. If you are interested in this, one of the best family-style resorts in the Pyrénées is **Hautacam** (*www.hautacam.com*), where children under six ski for free, and there are no black runs at all. The resort is not far from Lourdes, and has 26km (16 miles) of downhill slopes, as well as 15km (over 9 miles) for cross-

country skiing. Another good choice is **La Pierre Saint-Martin** (*www.lapierrestmartin.com*), which again offers a nursery for children who are too young to ski, allowing parents to enjoy the slopes. For those who are taking their first steps (or slides), the resort has a mini-club with snow animals, games and races to encourage children to get used to snow and skiing at their own pace.

A good way to get to know the ski resorts is to take the **Cirque de Lys cable car**. This leaves from the train station in Cauterets (which has its own ski resort), and travels over 36km (22 miles) of ski slopes and resorts. In the summer months, this is a great way to access some excellent walking routes.

And do remember that in France most people tend to take their holidays all at the same peak times, so be careful in mid-February, when the half-term break seems to attract endless hordes of French families and teenagers. And also bear in mind that snow can get a little thin on the ground in the lower resorts by April. To be certain of good conditions, you are best to try always to be above 1,000m (3,280ft) of altitude – although you've always got the luxurious alternative of thermal spas in almost all resorts in southwest France…

Pau and the foothills of the Pyrénées

At the foot of the Hautes-Pyrénées, Pau is often described as the most English town in France. There is a history of English military presence here, but the reputation stems from its staging of various English-style events, from horse racing, golf and lawn tennis to rugby and even fox hunting. Pau is the regional capital of the Béarn *département*, and was the birthplace of Henry IV. The key sites are the beautiful **Boulevard des Pyrénées** (with views over the Pic du Midi), the **Place Reine Margarite** (Pau's oldest square, dating from the 15th century) and the **Château de Pau**, where Henry was born, and which has not only beautiful formal gardens but also access to woods behind. Every June, the château courtyard and the Théâtre Saint-Louis host the Pau Festival.

Musée Bernadotte

A low-key but fascinating visit in Pau is to this authentic 18th-century house that belonged to a simple local soldier who grew up to become King of Sweden. Jean Baptiste Bernadotte was born in 1763 to a middle-class family and became a soldier at the age of 17. His career took off because after the French Revolution his lack of noble birth was no longer a hindrance to promotion, and he ended up becoming elected Prince Regent of Sweden, and then crowned King of Sweden and Norway in 1818. The present heads of the Swedish, Norwegian and Luxembourg royal families are descended from this ordinary French soldier.
rue Bernadotte. Tel: 05 59 27 48 42. Open: Tue–Sun 10am–noon & 2–6pm. Admission charge.

Musée National du Château de Pau

An excellent collection of tapestries plus ornate ceilings and chandeliers make this a lovely visit. There is also plenty of information, and re-creations of the life of Henry IV.
2 rue du Château. Tel: 05 59 82 38 19. www.musee-chateau-pau.fr. Open: summer daily 9.30am–12.30pm & 1.30–6.45pm; winter 9.30–11.45am &

Château de Pau

Bridge over the Gave de Pau at Orthez

*2–5pm; gardens are open 7.30am–dusk.
Free admission.*

Orthez

Just northwest of Pau, the beautiful town of Orthez has a 13th-century fortified bridge across the Gave de Pau river, once used as a commercial route for English and Flemish textiles, wool, olive oil and wine. Orthez also has several traditional stone houses, the last remaining tower of a 13th-century castle, and one of the few bullfighting arenas still left in southwest France. This controversial sport is nowhere near as popular in France as in Spain, but there are still a few approved schools and bullrings, and the festival of Orthez, held every July, hosts a bullfight alongside the concerts and other entertainments. In contrast to most Spanish bullfights, here the bulls are not (supposedly) fatally gored.

Petit Train d'Artouste

Around an hour away from Pau is the village of Fabrèges, where you can take a cable car into the Pyrénées. This train is the highest in Europe, climbing to 2,000m (6,560ft) in altitude up to the lake, Lac d'Artouste, where you can fish, swim, go boating or take one of the many hiking paths.
Tel: 05 59 05 49 61.
www.train-artouste.com.
Open: May–Sept. Admission charge.

Jurançon and Madiran

These are two wine regions within easy striking distance of Pau, with very different styles of wine. Madiran is home to the big, burly Tannat grape that makes long-lasting red wines, while Jurançon concentrates on white wines, both sweet and dry, mainly from the Gros Manseng and Petit Manseng grapes.

Flora and fauna in the mountains of the Pyrénées

The Pyrénées hide a vast array of animals, birds, plants and other wildlife, much of it extremely rare and even endangered. To get to know what is out there, you can explore the mountains by bike, car, canoe… even by abseiling or hang-gliding. But the best way to maximise your chances of meeting some of the rarest creatures in this stunning part of France is by taking a walk, armed with nothing more than a camera and a pair of binoculars, and gently allowing nature to unfold around you.

Strict protection is enforced in the central zone covering over 457sq km (176sq miles), and you can explore vast swathes of utterly unspoilt landscape,

The rare pyramidal orchid is native to the Pyrénées

with altitudes ranging from around 800m to 2,500m (2,620–8,200ft). There are several official companies that organise walking tours, and every local tourist office in the small villages will have maps showing the best local walking routes, with difficulty indicated. Whether you decide to take an official guide with you or just head out armed with a good (and up-to-date) map, just remember a strong pair of walking shoes, plenty of water and sunblock, and a pair of binoculars.

Among the rare species that you might be lucky enough to spot is the Pyrenean brown bear, which was hunted almost to extinction but has been the subject of intense conservation efforts (with some bears reintroduced in recent years from Slovenia in an attempt to boost the local population). There are thought to be around 30 bears living in the mountains today, and although some local farmers continue to be opposed to them because of dangers to their crops, efforts to increase numbers continue to be ever more successful, with the bears now tagged and tracked to ensure they stay safe. And don't worry – although pretty big, the bears are mostly vegetarian and are rarely aggressive. That said, as with any wild animal, never approach them – and you might want to bear in mind that a few walkers were charged by Pyrenean cows during the summer of 2010.

Another animal that has been brought back from the brink of disappearing in this part of the world is the marmot (a kind of large fluffy squirrel that looks distinctly like an over-fed domestic cat). They are now thought to number around 1,000 in the wilds of the mountains, and are often seen scampering happily across rocks with their brothers and sisters. Again though, no matter how sweet they look, don't be tempted to approach them.

In total, there are thought to be between 70 and 100 different animal species in the Pyrénées, among them mountain deer (particularly the very shy isard, often seen darting away across a seemingly sheer rock face), the natterjack toad which lives only at very high altitudes, Brebis sheep, mountain goats, foxes, pheasants and wild boar. Birds of prey are usually easy to spot, especially the golden eagles and peregrine falcons, plus the more eerie bearded vultures.

But animal numbers are dwarfed by the numbers of flowers and trees, again many of them highly unusual and rarely seen outside of this area, such as the Pyrenean iris and the blue thistle. Besides the forests of silver birch, pine and oak, there are hundreds of wild orchids which attract specialists from the world over, and thousands of butterflies that arrive to graze on them.

Toulouse and the Tarn

As you head to Toulouse, its immediate surrounds and the neighbouring Tarn district, the atmosphere changes. Everything here feels more exotic, more heated, more 'southern' than Bordeaux, the Gironde and Biarritz, as you move further away from the Atlantic Ocean and leave the cooling breezes of the mountains behind. In both Toulouse and the Tarn, you can feel that you are slipping towards the Languedoc, the Mediterranean, and the South of France.

This comes through in the landscape – expect to see fig, olive and cyprus trees alongside fields of sunflowers and lavender – but also in the heat (over 2,000 hours of sunshine per year is average in Toulouse) and in the laid-back, friendly atmosphere. Eating happens later here, siestas start to creep in during the hot midday hours, and the whole of life seems to shift outside for the summer months. Over in the Tarn, where the main cities are Albi and Gaillac and the Tarn river replaces the Garonne, the ever-important vines are punctuated with other forms of agriculture, and outdoor festivals and farmers' markets are the order of the day. Allow yourself to shift down a gear when exploring these regions, and be prepared for the unexpected.

TOULOUSE
The city
The capital city of the Midi-Pyrénées, Toulouse is imbued with a warm, southern spirit. The aeronautics industry has made Toulouse one of the most dynamic cities in France, with the fastest-growing population of any major French city, and one of the very few to be completely solvent, with no national debt! Known as 'La Ville Rose' (The Pink City) because of the soft red brick of its buildings, the city is split fairly neatly by the Garonne river, with the Old Town on the Right Bank, full of winding pedestrianised streets and countless ancient churches and museums. The Left Bank is more modern and artistic, with a large student population, several outdoor markets and increasingly hip neighbourhood bars and restaurants. Toulouse also has some of the best shopping and nightlife of southwest France, with a young feel due to its large university population, and a lively and successful contemporary arts scene.

Les Abattoirs
Housed in a huge brick building that was used as an abattoir in the 19th

Toulouse and the Tarn

century, this contemporary art gallery has cavernous rooms that lend themselves to impressive displays. The whole collection comprises over 2,000 works (including paintings, installations, sculpture, mixed- and multimedia) by artists from 44 countries, from Picasso to modern-day emerging artists. It has a genuinely exciting feel, and a good café! *76 allée Charles de Fitte. Tel: 05 62 48 58 00. www.lesabattoirs.org. Open: summer Wed–Sun 11am–7pm; winter Wed–Fri 10am–6pm, Sat & Sun 11am–7pm. Admission charge. Bus: 1. Metro: Saint-Cyprien République.*

Basilique Saint-Sernin

The Romanesque basilica, dating from 1096, is one of Toulouse's most famous and beautiful sights. Its outstanding feature is the Porte Miegeville, decorated with 12th-century sculptures. Concerts are often held here.
Place Saint-Sernin. Tel: 05 61 21 80 45. Open: daily 8.30–11.30am & 2–5.30pm. Bus: Navette Tisseo.

Le Bazacle

A strange mix of working power station and art gallery – don't think about it too much, just enjoy one of the best views of the Garonne river in the city.
11 quai Saint-Pierre. Tel: 05 62 30 16 00. Open: Tue–Fri 2–7pm (Tue–Sun during exhibitions). Free admission. Bus: Navette Tisseo.

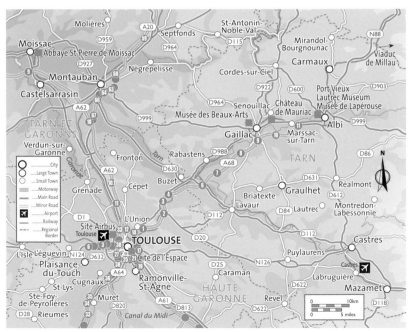

Canal du Midi

Central Toulouse is an easy access point for the canal that stretches from just above the city, around the city centre, then right down to Sète on the Mediterranean coast. Originally conceived as a short cut between the Atlantic and the Mediterranean, it has 103 locks, plus bridges, dams and a tunnel. One of the best access points is the Port de l'Embouchure, dating from 1667. Three picturesque bridges span the waterways, and at the reservoir you can view a marble engraving of life on the river. You can experience the canal by strolling along it or taking a boat trip, available through **NaviCanal** (*www.navicanal.com*).

Cité de l'Espace (Space City)

Here you'll find a full-scale Mir space station (once used by the Russians), an

The Augustins' tower

CASSOULET

Probably the most famous food to come out of Toulouse (after the sausage), a classic cassoulet (a rich, slow-cooked bean casserole) will make full use of the local pork sausages (but may also be substituted by mutton or duck), mixed with pork skin (couenne) and white haricot beans. The dish is named after the cassole, the distinctive oval covered earthenware pot in which cassoulet is traditionally cooked. When preparing it, it is traditional to use the pot from the previous cassoulet in order to give a base for the next one – so in theory just having one endless pot on the go. Many restaurants have their own versions. In the city centre, **La Cave au Cassoulet** (*54 rue Peyrolières. Tel: 05 56 13 60 30*) claims to be the most authentic.

Ariane 5 rocket and a children's space base that allows you to learn about gravity, building and launching a rocket, and testing a space sleeping bag. There is also a more serious museum section about the solar system and space travel. All in all, this makes for a highly enjoyable day out and is a real must-see when in Toulouse. *Parc de la Plaine, Avenue Jean Gonord. Tel: 05 62 71 48 71. www.cite-espace.com. Open: Mon–Fri 9am–6pm, weekends 9am–7pm. Access via Périphérique Est de Toulouse, exit 17 or 18. Bus: 19 stops outside, 35 close by. Admission charge.*

Musée des Augustins

This beautiful, peaceful space has an exhibition of Renaissance paintings and artefacts, with sculptures from the Middle Ages. From within the museum,

The Capitole

you can also access the 14th-century church and cloister.
21 rue de Metz. Tel: 05 61 22 21 82. Open: Thur–Mon 10am–6pm, Wed 10am–9pm. Closed: Tue. Admission charge. Metro: Esquirol.

Place du Capitole
Toulouse's handsome central square, with the 250-year-old Capitole as its centrepiece. Although the square is often lively and packed, make sure you stop to admire the eight red marble columns representing the eight *capitouls* (magistrates) of the municipality. Inside the Capitole itself, there are frescoes and various monuments to illustrious past residents of the city.
Metro: Capitole.

Place de la Daurade
Great fun during the summer, this is a beach in the middle of the city, right on the banks of the Garonne by the Pont Neuf (New Bridge). It's the place to people-spot young Toulousians.
Metro: Esquirol, then a ten-minute walk.

Taxiway (Site Airbus)
The largest aeronautical site in Europe is open to visitors by prior appointment. You can tour both the double-decker Airbus and a model of the original Concorde.
Taxiway, 10 avenue Guynemer, 31770 Colomiers. Tel: 05 61 18 06 01. www.taxiway.fr. Open: Mon–Sat, booking essential. Train: Gare de Colomiers. Car: 10km (6¼ miles) from Toulouse along A624. Admission charge.

Walk: Toulouse

This walk provides a fascinating and unusual view of Toulouse, following the city's river and green spaces. Covering around 5km (3 miles), the walk should take three or four hours at a gentle pace, but there are several points along the route where you can cut it short or extend it, as you wish.

Start at Le Grand Rond, a large public park that is also at the meeting point of the city's main boulevards.

1 Le Jardin des Plantes (Botanical Gardens)

Created at the time of the French Revolution, this is the oldest public park in Toulouse, with over 100 different species of trees and conifers. There's plenty to do here with little ones, from pony trekking to go-karting. *Allée Frederic Mistral. Open: 7.45am–dusk. Bus: 92.*

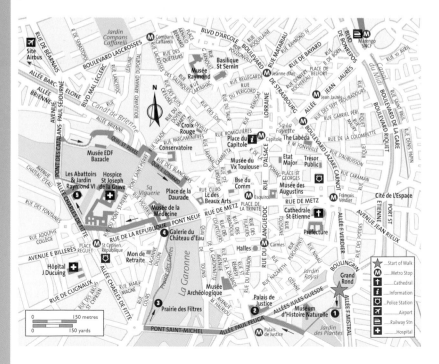

Come out at the rue Alfred Dumeril exit, and cross over allées Jules Guesde to the Palais de Justice.

2 Palais de Justice (Courthouse)

This strikingly modern building has been the subject of much excitement in Toulouse in recent years, as during restorations it was found to be the site of medieval vestiges of a castle belonging to the Comte de Toulouse: Château Narbonnais. Viewing points are made possible via a system of raised walkways, and the tourist office runs visits once a week. From 2011, a more comprehensive public access museum is due to open.

From here, turn right and continue down allées Jules Guesde and over Pont Saint-Michel. You can at this point turn into the avenue du Grand Ramier and explore the Île du Ramier, with its pool, sports fields, music and exhibition centres. Or continue across the bridge to another green space.

3 Prairie des Filtres (literally 'Filters Meadow')

This long, thin park sits along the banks of the Garonne looking back over the attractive waterfront of the Old Town. Opened in 1976, it is a perfect picnic spot, and often hosts outdoor markets and concerts.

Walk through the park and up on to the Pont Neuf, where you'll find an art gallery housed in a circular former water tower.

4 Galerie du Château d'Eau (Château d'Eau Photographers Gallery)

One of Toulouse's most unusual galleries, dedicated to contemporary photography.

1 place Laganne. Tel: 05 61 77 09 40. www.galeriechateaudeau.org. Open: Tue–Sun 1–7pm. Admission charge.

Cross the Pont Neuf (you can return to the Old Town at this point by simply crossing the bridge) and walk down rue Viguerie, where you can stop to admire the architecture and gardens of the Hôtel-Dieu Saint-Jacques hospital. Turn down rue Saint-Nicolas and then left from Pont Saint-Pierre down to allée Charles De Fitte.

5 Les Abattoirs and Jardin Raymond VI

Right on the banks of the Garonne, behind Les Abattoirs modern art museum (*see pp88–9*), this is one of the liveliest city parks, full every weekend with families enjoying the large children's play area and spilling out from the gallery to enjoy the view of the river, as water cascades over the weir. Good jogging and cycling paths.

From here, cross over Pont des Catalans back to the Old Town. You can choose to extend your walk by exploring the Bazacle (see p89) or wander back along the Quai Saint-Pierre and Quai Lombard into the centre of town.

TOULOUSE ENVIRONS AND THE TARN

The area around Toulouse is home to some of the most interesting and distinctive wines in France, which richly reward taking the time to explore them. These are usually made with grape varieties that are known only in their particular area, often following practices that have been handed down through the generations and continue to be very much family-focused. The wines of Madiran and Jurançon are also often grouped with the wines of the Toulouse area, but are geographically closer to Pau and Lourdes (*see p85*). Over here you will find rustic winemakers who are more than happy to open their doors to you and demonstrate how to best pair their wines with the hearty local food.

Typical Garonne canal boats

The Tarn – and Aveyron, which also touches this part of the southwest – is also host to a wealth of architectural treasures, from the 2,000-year-old city of Albi to the ultra-modern lines of the Milau Viaduct, and holds plenty of attractions for non-wine lovers. The Tarn *département* has approximately 2,380 hours of sunshine annually, with temperatures rising to 40°C (104°F), and has four beautiful rivers (the Tarn, the Viaur, the Cérou and the Agout) in which to canoe, kayak, sail and swim. Its geographical position, between the Massif Central and the Pyrénées, and on the route between the Atlantic and the Mediterranean, also means it has been the site of various disputes and land-grabs over the centuries, resulting in the many bastide towns, fortified historic monuments and castles everywhere.

Albi

Albi is the capital of the Tarn region, and a very attractive town with a gorgeous cathedral, good restaurants and wide streets. The entire place is rich in architectural history, and built with Languedoc-style red brick, as is Toulouse, giving it the same warm and welcoming feel. Besides its cathedral, Albi is best known as the birthplace of the painter Toulouse-Lautrec, and as you would expect – besides the excellent museum – many of its bars and restaurants feature frescoes of Moulin Rouge dancers. In fact, many restaurants also offer versions of dishes

Medieval half-timbered building, Albi

created by Lautrec, as he was also a keen amateur chef.

Albi Grand Prix

In September of every year, Albi gives itself over to race fever. This Grand Prix has been running for over 70 years and features car, motorcycle and rally events.
Tourist office, place Sainte-Cécile.
Tel: 05 63 49 48 98.
www.circuit-albi.com

Albi Jazz Festival

Held in June every year, this is a popular jazz festival where many events are held throughout the city. A classical music festival is held over the last two weeks of July, also on an annual basis.
Tourist office, place Sainte-Cécile.
Tel: 05 63 49 48 98.

Cathédrale Sainte-Cécile

This huge cathedral is built like a fortress, imposing itself over the surrounding city with its expanse of red brick. When illuminated at night, it's hard to tear your eyes away. But inside it's full of delicate Renaissance paintings, gorgeous carved screens and huge stained-glass windows. It's also worth paying the small admission fee to go into the Grand Choeur for its frescoes.
Place Sainte-Cécile. Open: Jun–Sept
daily 8.30am–6.45pm; Oct–May
9am–noon & 2–6.30pm.

Musée Lapérouse
(Lapérouse Museum)

A man with a fascinating story that has its roots in Albi, Jean-François Galaup de Lapérouse was born in the city in

1741 and became a sailor by the age of 15, rising to eventually be declared captain in the French navy after proving his worth against the British troops during the American War of Independence. So highly regarded was he that he was eventually asked by Louis XVI to explore the New World for him, and he set off for Alaska, China, Russia and Australia with a crew of over 225 men – a voyage from which he never returned. This museum looks not only at his life, but also at the wider role that France played during these years. *41 rue Porta. Tel: 05 63 46 01 87. www.laperouse-france.fr. Open: Jul–Aug daily 9am–noon & 2–6pm; rest of the year Tue–Sun only. Admission charge.*

Musée Toulouse-Lautrec (Toulouse-Lautrec Museum)
Henri de Toulouse-Lautrec (1864–1901) was born in Albi to one of France's oldest aristocratic families, who were later probably a little shocked by his portrayal of the decadent modern lifestyle. Despite his being most closely associated with the Montmartre district of Paris, it seems only right that over 500 examples of his work, from early pencil sketches right up to the famous Paris brothel scenes he painted towards the end of his life, have returned to a permanent exhibition in his home town. He himself returned there, in ill-health in the 1880s, for treatments at the local

Toulouse-Lautrec Museum

spa towns. His many health problems, combined with his alcoholism, led to his early death at just 36. Lautrec is still a highly relevant artist today: one of his early paintings was sold at Christie's in 2005 for US$22.5 million. Once you have finished admiring his work, there's a very pretty park next door to the museum that is perfect for a stroll.

Place Sainte-Cécile. Tel: 05 63 49 48 70. www.musee-toulouse-lautrec.com. Open: Sept–Jun 9am–noon & 2–6pm; Jul–Aug 9am–6pm.

Port Vieux

This arched bridge over the Tarn river has been in existence since 1035, although it has obviously seen various restoration projects since the 11th century. A perfect photo spot.

Cordes-sur-Ciel

You'll hear about the medieval bastide of Cordes-sur-Ciel as soon as you get anywhere near the Tarn region, as pretty much everyone you meet will ask if you have been there yet. As the name suggests (Cordes in the Sky), it sits high above the surrounding countryside, clinging to the top of a hill, and can indeed look as if it is floating in the clouds. The bastide was built in the early 13th century by Comte de Toulouse Raimond VII, and has been inhabited pretty much ever since by a collection of artisans, furniture makers, artists, jewellers… and they've made a beautiful example of it. There is even a

Porte Medievale, Cordes-sur-Ciel

local wine, a dry, lightly sparkling white. Other medieval bastides, while you're in the area, include Castelnau-de-Montmiral, Puycelci and Penne.

Jardin des Paradis (Garden of Paradise)

A contemporary, Japanese-inspired garden in the middle of Cordes with a gorgeous mix of flowers, vegetables and quiet meditative corners.

Place du Theron. Tel: 05 63 56 29 77. www.cordes-sur-ciel.org. Open: Apr–Jun daily 2–5pm; Jul–Aug 10.30am–7pm; Sept–Oct 2–6pm.

Musée de l'Art du Sucre (Museum of the Art of Sugar)

Sugar fanatics ahoy – this might just be the high point of your holiday.

Renowned chef Yves Thuriès has been creating his stunning patisseries here since 1988, and opened this museum and workshop just a year later. You can feast (just your eyes, sadly) upon creations of spun sugar and learn the techniques behind them. Several award-winning pastry and patisserie chefs can also be found here throughout the year, usually sharpening up their skills before an international competition. A workshop in the art of sugar is also available if you book ahead.
Haut de la Cité. Tel: 05 63 56 02 40. www.artdusucre.fr. Open: mid-Jun–mid-Sept daily 10.30am–12.30pm & 1.30–7pm; Apr–mid-Jun & mid-Sept–Nov Tue–Sun 10.30am–12.30pm & 1.30–6pm. Admission charge.

Gaillac

The town of Gaillac is gorgeous, with large cobbled squares, elegant bridges over the River Tarn, and a very attractive Maison du Vin. This is a big wine region, with winemaking dating from the 1st century. Today, it is little known on the international scene but one of the most developed in France in terms of receiving visitors, with an organised wine route that is well signposted and full of welcoming characters.

Château de Mauriac

The classical painter Bernard Bistes was born in Albi (*see 'Art in Albi', pp100–101*) but now lives in this stunning property surrounded by Gaillac vineyards. Inside there is a mix of classic portraits and

furniture from the Renaissance, alongside the artist's own work.
81600 Senouillac. Tel: 05 63 41 71 18. www.bistes.com. Open: May–Oct daily 3–6pm; rest of the year by appointment only. Admission charge.

Musée des Beaux-Arts (Fine Arts Museum)

Wide-ranging exhibits from contemporary sculptures to Romantic painters are set in a lovely château with formal Italian-style gardens.
Château de Foucard, avenue Dom Vayssette. Tel: 05 63 57 18 25. Open: May–Sept Wed–Mon 10am–noon & 2–6pm; Oct–Apr Fri–Sun 10am–noon & 2–6pm. Admission charge.

Viaduc de Millau (Millau Viaduct)

The Millau Viaduct, or Suspension Bridge, is in the Aveyron *département*, on the edge of the Tarn, and is just nudging out of southwest France, but architecture fans might be willing to take the detour. Built by English architect Norman Foster, with French engineering expert Michel Virlogeux, it has been open since December 2004 and is 2,460m (8,070ft) wide, and reaches up to 343m (1,125ft) high (that's 19m/62ft higher than the Eiffel Tower in Paris). There are several suggested spots in the region for viewing the bridge, but one of the most enjoyable is the attractive village of Peyre, around 7km (4¼ miles) from the bridge.
A75 motorway. www.leviaducdemillau.com

Abbaye Saint-Pierre de Moissac (Moissac Abbey of St Peter)

This UNESCO World Heritage Site is a recognised stop on the Saint Jacques de Compostela route, and dates from the 12th century (when it was affiliated to Cluny abbey in Burgundy). It is also a centre of Romanesque art and a documentation centre for medieval literature and sculpture. Its cloisters are renowned for being among the most beautiful in France.

Allées de Brienne, 82200 Moissac. Tel: 05 63 04 41 79. Train to Moissac station. North of Toulouse, around 30 minutes from Montauban.

The Viaduc de Millau

Toulouse and the Tarn

Art in Albi

As the birthplace of not only Toulouse-Lautrec but also renowned modern artists such as Bernard Bistes (a classical painter who now works from the Château de Mauriac in Gaillac, *see p98*), it's not surprising that Albi continues to sustain and develop its artistic heritage. It's also not hard to see how culture can flourish here – the very walls of the city seem to encourage it, starting with the UNESCO World Heritage area of the Cité Épiscopale (Episcopal City) at the heart of the Old Town, with its perfectly preserved 13th-century Sainte-Cécile cathedral and archbishop's palace, Le Palais de la Berbie. Next to these, the Pont Vieux (Old Bridge, aptly named considering it is now almost exactly 1,000 years old) and the stone ramparts continue to exude this sense of timelessness, and just by strolling around these landmarks you can easily imagine the creative influence they have exerted over the centuries.

Throughout the year, a series of festivals is held celebrating the arts, from rock, classical and jazz music festivals to large-scale book and theatre fairs. Apparently even fashion designer Jean Paul Gaultier has been moved to purchase a holiday property in this attractive red-bricked town, finding an apartment in a run-down riverside building that has been fully restored over the past few years.

Other artistic events are more permanent, such as the many museums and galleries that are tucked among the city's streets. One of the most unusual artistic institutions – and largely responsible for Albi's reputation as one of the leading artistic centres in France – is the **Laboratoire Artistique International du Tarn** (International Artistic Laboratory of the Tarn), more commonly known as LAIT. This is a gallery and studio space that encourages young and emerging artists working in any discipline, whether paint, photography, sculpture, multimedia or film. The idea is to give them the space (and the funds) to establish themselves and their work. It has been described as a 'cultural think-tank' by several French journalists, due to its collaborative and fearless approach, but it also aims to be very much part of the local community. Funded by a mix of private and public money, the venue is an exhibition space and learning centre offering workshops, talks, debates and exhibitions to the visiting public, who are encouraged to get as involved as they like by learning artistic techniques themselves. There are residential courses run throughout the year in different disciplines from modelmaking to life drawing, and regular classes such as those that introduce the idea of understanding and interpreting modern art to school-children through gallery visits and discussion groups. To show how seriously fostering new talent is taken here, once a year an Artist in Residence is given a grant to spend ten months developing a project at the centre, in conjunction with the wider town of Albi, and to then run an exhibition of their work for two months over the following summer for the public to enjoy – and for them to increase their exposure and experience as an artist. Each year, a competition process is held to select the next artist, with winners coming both from France and further afield. *Exhibitions are held at Moulin Albigeois, 41 rue Porta. Tel: 05 63 38 35 91. www.centredartlelait.com. Open: Wed–Sun 2–7pm. Admission charge.*

Gardens of the Toulouse-Lautrec Museum, Albi

The Dordogne and the Lot

The green heart of southwest France, these two départements *have long attracted visitors drawn by the gentle, easy pace of life, the abundance of natural produce, and the traditional stone villages set beside the beautiful rivers of the Dordogne and the Lot. The Dordogne, or Le Périgord as this area is also known, covers four regions that are differentiated by the colours of their landscape.*

There is Purple Périgord around Bergerac (so named for its wine), Green Périgord (the wildest section) to the north of the region around the Val de Dronne and the national park, White Périgord around the city of Périgueux (named after its chalky soils), and Black Périgord (around Sarlat, so-called for its abundance of truffles). A little further south, the Lot stretches down through Figeac, Rocamadour and Puy-l'Évêque to the medieval city of Cahors.

Both regions contain wonderful national parks: the Causses du Quercy in the Lot, and the Périgord-Limousin in the Dordogne, just touching the northern section of the region, and filled with walking, cycling and hiking routes. And both regions have stunning examples of work by prehistoric man, from the cliffs where they lived to the cave drawings that they left behind. All in all, there is plenty to explore in these fascinating regions of France that have cast generations of visitors under their spell.

Bergerac and Périgueux, both with airports and good rail and road links, form the most usual points of access into the region, but they are also architectural and historical treasures in their own right.

TRUFFLE MARKETS

The black truffle (*Tuber melanosporum*) is one of the culinary treasures of both the Dordogne and the Lot. The traditional truffle-hunting pigs have been largely replaced by dogs (who are less likely to eat their finds), but you can still join them on truffle hunts if you're lucky. Black rather than white truffles are found here and are most usually unearthed over the winter months. Or to guarantee you can get hold of them, try visiting one of the many truffle markets, held out in Sainte-Alvère on Monday mornings, or further out in Périgord in the village of Sorges (known as the Truffle Capital of the Dordogne). In the Lot, the main truffles market is held in the town of Lalbenque. The delicacies are at their peak in January, when a truffle festival is also held.

For more information, visit the Bergerac tourist office, 97 rue Neuve d'Argenson.
Tel: 05 53 57 03 11.

THE DORDOGNE
Bergerac
Vieux Port (Old Port)

You can take a traditional flat-bottomed *gabare* boat from the pretty riverside of the Old Port in Bergerac. From here you can easily walk up the slope towards the Maison des Vins, and then behind it into the pedestrianised streets of the Old Town. Don't forget to explore the cloisters in the Maison des Vins, which used to be monks' cells but are now the site of several art and photography exhibitions held throughout the year.

Maison des Vins, 1 rue des Récollets, Quai Salvette. Tel: 05 53 63 57 55. www.vins-bergerac.fr. Open: daily 9am–7pm.

Périgueux
Église Saint-Étienne-de-la-Cité

A stunning Romanesque church (it was a cathedral until the mid-17th century) that has been partly destroyed but contains a huge 11th-century dome that is the largest in the Périgord region. The cathedral of Saint-Front is the far more visited site in town – and its beautiful Romanesque-meets-Byzantine building is certainly striking – but this smaller church has its own special charms.

10 avenue Cavaignac. Tel: 05 53 06 48 10. Open: daily 10am–6pm.

Farmers' markets

The Dordogne is bursting with fresh-produce farmers' markets, and one of

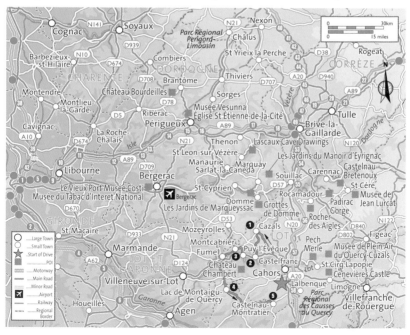

the best is held in Périgueux at the Place du Coderc almost every morning of the week. Night markets are also held on Wednesday nights in July and August. *Place du Coderc. Open: Tue–Sun 6am–1pm.*

Vesunna, Musée Gallo-Romain (Gallo-Roman Museum)

The epicentre of Roman Périgueux, this museum building was designed by architect Jean Nouvel, and looks at daily life in the city from the 1st to the 3rd centuries AD. The original Roman walled city was known as Vesunna, named after the Vésone spring found near the original site.
Parc de Vésone, 20 rue du 26ème Régiment d'Infanterie. Tel: 05 53 53 00 92. www.vesunna.fr

Brantôme

Known rather optimistically as the Venice of Périgord, this is a highly attractive town, with cobblestone streets, a beautiful stone bridge across the River Dronne, and steep wooded slopes around the town. There is also a beautiful abbey and several good boutiques. Nearby is the smaller and less crowded Saint-Jean-de-Cole, an attractive 11th-century village with a Roman church, and the Dolmen de Peyrelevade, a preserved megalithic monument worth visiting.

Château Bourdeilles

Also close to Brantôme, and lying along the River Dronne, this attractive

château is the site of several concerts, dinners and exhibitions throughout the year. The town of Bourdeilles itself is likewise worth stopping at.
24310 Bourdeilles. www.bourdeilles.com. Open: Jun–Sept daily 9.30am–12.30pm & 2–6pm; Oct–May Wed–Mon.

Les Jardins de Marqueyssac

A wonderful visit for garden lovers, these are known as the Hanging Gardens of Marqueyssac. They are set high on a ridge (at 192m/630ft) overlooking the Dordogne valley, and cover 6km (3¾ miles) of shady walkways and stunning viewpoints.
24220 Veyzac. Tel: 05 53 31 36 36. www.marqueyssac.com. Open: Jul–Aug daily 9am–8pm; Apr–Jun & Sept–Oct 9am–7pm; rest of the year see website. Admission charge.

Sarlat-la-Canéda

Sarlat has been somewhat a victim of its own success in recent years, but if you can grab a quiet day in any month outside July and August, you will be reminded of just why this is seen as one of the architectural jewels of the Dordogne, with its medieval centre and houses, Roman and Gothic architecture, and seemingly countless art galleries and tiny museums.

Gorodka

This contemporary art centre has been going for 40 years, based in a forest just 4km (2½ miles) outside of Sarlat. There are several walking circuits through the forest that take you past art installations, and eight galleries with more permanent collections of around 400 works of art.

24200 Sarlat-la-Canéda. Tel: 05 53 31 02 00. Email: info@gorodka.com. www.gorodka.com. A navette goes from Sarlat to the village of La Canéda, then it's a very short walk (all signposted).

PERCHED VILLAGES, GROTTOES AND GORGES

Set high up on promontories all over the Dordogne and the Lot, these villages originally grew up because of their defensive possibilities. Most typically, a perched village is laid out in two separate areas: one at the riverside, one on the cliff top above. The highest part of the villages will almost always have various religious and historical monuments that will have attracted

pilgrims for centuries travelling along the Santiago de Compostela route.

Today the pilgrims are replaced by tourists, but the other-worldly allure remains as strong as ever, and almost all have artisan workshops and plenty of good restaurants and cafés, not to mention gorges, caves and grottoes that lie beneath.

Some of the most interesting are:

Beynac

The château of Beynac, perched on its limestone cliff, dominates the town of the same name and is one of the most distinctive sites in the Dordogne – it has been used as a setting for various films, including Luc Besson's *Jeanne d'Arc* in 1999. Inside the castle, there are beautiful tapestries hung on the walls and an excellent re-creation of life in the Middle Ages. In the rest of the town, just enjoy the tiny paved streets,

Château de Beynac

the 12th-century chapel and the attractive port on the riverbanks below. *www.beynac-en-perigord.com*

Castelnau-Bretenoux

This 13th-century castle stands on a rocky spur above the Dordogne valley, 38km (24 miles) from Rocamadour. *46130 Prudhomat. Tel: 05 65 10 98 00. Open: Jul–Aug daily 10am–7pm; Jun 10am–12.30pm & 2–6.30pm; rest of the year see website. Admission charge.*

Domme

Dating from 1281, this medieval bastide town is the site of the Graffiti Templiers and the Prison des Templiers, where you can still see 14th-century graffiti on the walls, written by Knights Templar inmates. *www.ot-domme.com*

Grottes de Domme

You enter these limestone caves via the 17th-century town hall and go underground through 450m (1,480ft) of grottoes. A panoramic lift brings you back up, affording stunning views over the Dordogne valley. *Place de la Halle. Tel: 05 53 31 71 00. Open: Jul–Aug daily 10am–6.30pm; Jun & Sept 10am–noon & 2–6pm; rest of the year 10am–noon & 2.30–4.30pm. Admission charge.*

THE LOT
Padirac

The gorge and grottoes of Padirac are one of the stellar attractions of the

region and should not be missed. The Gouffre de Padirac is a natural 75m-deep (246ft) chasm, below which a river flows at a depth of 103m (338ft) underground. *Tel: 05 65 33 64 56. www.gouffre-de-padirac.com. Open: Aug daily 8.30am–6.30pm; rest of the year see website. Visits last around 90 minutes and cover 2,000m (6,560ft). Admission charge.*

Rocamadour

Just over the border in the Lot, this is one of the best known of the perched villages, attracting well over a million visitors per year. The medieval village still has well-preserved ramparts, as well as the celebrated sanctuary with its complex of monastic buildings. Expect plenty of cafés, restaurants, ice-cream parlours and gift shops – but somehow still a sense of authenticity and calm.

www.rocamadour.com

Rocher des Aigles (Eagle Rock)

Just outside Rocamadour is this eagle sanctuary, where you can see around 400 different birds, and around 60 different species, including falcons, eagles, parrots, condors and vultures. Visitors can walk around, take guided tours, or watch one of the many daily displays of falconry or even bald-eagle fishing. *Le Château, 46500 Rocamadour. Tel: 05 65 33 65 45. www.rocherdesaigles.com. Open: Jul–Aug daily 11am–7pm; Jun & Sept 1–6pm; rest of the year see website. Admission charge.*

Rocamadour

Saint-Céré

Set high on a promontory in the Lot region, dominated by the ruins of the Château de Saint-Laurent-les-Tours, this village has incredible views over the surrounding countryside.

www.tourisme-saint-cere.com

Musée de Jean Lurçat

Lurçat was one of the key figures in the French Resistance during World War II, and ran most of his operations from his base in southwest France. He was also an artist, and after the war moved to this studio just outside Saint-Céré. It is now a museum of his work, with his painting, pottery and drawings all arranged in the rooms where he lived, making this a really charming visit.

46400 Saint-Laurent-les-Tours.
Tel: 05 65 38 28 21. Open: Jul–Sept daily
9.30–noon & 2.30–6.30pm.
Admission charge.

Saint-Cirq-Lapopie

The village of Saint-Cirq-Lapopie is perched on a cliff 100m (330ft) above the river and is one of the major beauty spots of the Lot valley. Very close to the prehistoric remains at the Grotte de Pech Merle (*see p109*), it provides easy access to various hiking routes, as well as canoeing down the river. For a quieter experience, simply look out over the valley from the ruins of the fortress ramparts.

www.saint-cirqlapopie.com

Souillac

Sitting to the east of Sarlat, this riverside town (not strictly a perched village, but set in the heart of them, and right on the riverside) is known for its beautiful viaduct and arched bridge, and the Abbaye Sainte-Marie (Saint Mary's Abbey).

www.tourisme-souillac.com

The Lascaux cave paintings

The most famous teenagers in France, one war-torn summer back in 1940, were called Marcel, Jacques, Georges and Simon. When out walking one day, they – along with Marcel's dog Robot – stumbled across one of the greatest archaeological finds of the past century, and took the country's mind off the war for a welcome moment. What they had found were near-perfect cave paintings by early man, with over 2,000 images in a series of seven underground caverns, dating from the Palaeolithic era and thought to be over 17,000 years old. The cave's fame quickly spread beyond France, and it remains the subject of intense study by archaeologists to this day. The entrance to the grotto that the boys discovered sits at 185m (605ft) above sea level, overlooking the Lascaux valley. Contained within it, there are over 6,000 representations of animals at Lascaux – mainly horses, but also stags, ibexes and bison. There are few pictures of humans, just one full image of a human figure, although many of individual parts (usually a hand or arm in a hunting scene).

These remain the most famous cave paintings in France, opened to the public in 1948 but closed off since 1963 because of worries over damage to the delicate paintings through sheer numbers of visitors. Their breathing alone was affecting the paintings, producing large amounts of carbon dioxide. The paintings have since been restored to their original state, and a replica of two of the cave halls opened nearby the original in 1983. This is what you can visit today, but in recent years, even the replica caves have been suffering from the vast numbers of crowds who flock here every year (*www.lascaux.culture.fr*).

To avoid causing further damage, it's worth knowing that there are other less well-known sites throughout the Vézère valley, which is thought to contain 147 prehistoric sites in total, covering around 350,000 years of history, together with 25 decorated caves. Further away still, the Lot has several important historical sites that can offer a far more satisfying experience, with fewer queues and greater access to the paintings. Among these are Saint-Léon-sur-Vézère, Marquay, Manaurie-Rouffignac, Font-de-Gaume, Bernifal and Pech Merle.

The discoveries across this region of France are easily among the richest worldwide, and have helped scholars, artists and writers form much of our picture of life as it was lived by our ancestors – from the tools used to carve and paint the images, to the scenes depicted in them of hunting, eating, celebrating and religious or spiritual rites. The reasons for the density of prehistoric remains in this area are thought to lie partly in its geology – namely great cracks in the rocks that allowed people to live safely within them, but sufficiently solid that they have remained intact for thousands of years.

Pech Merle, in the Lot valley, is a cave which opens onto a hillside at Cabrerets around 30 minutes from Cahors, and is one of the few original prehistoric cave painting sites in France that remain open to the general public. Discovered in 1922, so earlier than Lascaux, the caves extend for many kilometres underground, and about 1km (just over ½ a mile) from the entrance, you'll find deep caverns painted with dramatic murals dating from an estimated 25,000 years ago. This site was used over thousands of years, and other paintings are thought to date from 16,000 years ago. There is also an excellent museum.
46330 Cabrerets. Tel: 05 65 31 27 05. www.pechmerle.com. Open: daily 9.30am–5pm. Admission charge.

Cave painting at Lascaux

Cahors

As the Dordogne slips into the Lot valley, the pace of life slows down even further. Truffles still reign here, and the vines are still ever-present – Cahors was one of the most famous wines in the world in the Middle Ages, and has been experiencing a recent renaissance as its Malbec grape becomes ever-more sought after. But the poor soils of the Lot bear little other agriculture, and most farming is centred around livestock, ducks (this is prime *foie gras* country), logging and fishing.

Cahors is the capital of the Lot region and is surrounded on three sides by the river. There are remains of the original Gallo-Roman city in the Arc de Diane (vestiges of the Roman baths), and the stunning Pont Valentré (nicknamed The Devil's Bridge), dating from the 14th century, is the only fortified bridge with three towers in the world and is a classified UNESCO site. The Cathédrale Saint-Étienne (Saint Stephen's Cathedral) is equally beautiful, with two large domes rising above it. It is especially good to visit on market days (Wednesday and Saturday mornings), when the Place Chapou right next to the cathedral positively buzzes with action.

Cahors is currently undertaking an indepth study into the archaeological remains of the town, and the next few years should see a number of new exhibitions opening up. But take some time simply to enjoy being in this charming place. Cahors can be explored at leisure, as it has a relaxed atmosphere and plenty of stopping-off points for those spending a day walking around. For the best pavement cafés, head to Boulevard Gambetta. The borders of the river have recently been restored and there is now a path all around the city.

Fontaine des Chartreux (Chartreux Spring)

Most probably this is the origin of the Gallo-Roman city of Cahors. It was part of a large water system in the old city, which included an aqueduct and thermal baths. To get to it, cross to the east side of the river, south of the Pont Valentré.

Hôtel de Roaldès

This beautiful half-timbered house belonged to the religious aristocracy and rich merchants during the late 15th century. Henri IV is said to have lived here during the siege of Cahors in 1580. Constructed of timber and brick, it has an upstairs gallery for enjoying the good weather (like in Venice), and a tower. *Place Henri IV, Quai Champollion. Tel: 05 65 53 20 65.*

Mont Saint-Cyr (Saint Cyr Peak)

You'll have to face a winding and pretty hair-raising drive to get up here, but the view from the top, over the whole expanse of Cahors, is well worth it. From here you can clearly see the Old Town and its main tree-lined street running north to south. The three lovely bridges are also visible. The peak of Saint Cyr stands at 260m (850ft) above sea level, and there is also a small restaurant where you can reward yourself for the effort expended.

Musée de Cahors Henri-Martin (Henri Martin Museum)

This houses a highly comprehensive collection of paintings, sculptures and artefacts that date from prehistory through to the present day. Various permanent and visiting exhibitions take you through the history of the area from prehistory through to Gallo-Roman and medieval times, right through the Renaissance and up to today, with some excellent photography and video exhibits. Henri Martin was a painter from Toulouse, at his peak

Pont Valentré, Cahors

during the late 19th and early 20th centuries, and several of his paintings are also exhibited here.

792 rue Émile Zola. Tel: 05 65 20 88 66. www.mairie-cahors.fr/musee.
Open: Mon & Wed–Sat 11am–6pm, Sun 2–6pm. Closed: Tue.
Admission charge.

Musée de la Résistance (Resistance Museum)

You could say there are quite a few Resistance Museums across southwest France, but this was the heartland of the fight for Free France. The exhibition details the battle across the Lot region, the bombing of railway lines and hiding of Allied troops, but it also looks at the wider story of World War II. The museum opened in 1992, and each room is dedicated to a local hero who died during the conflict.

Place Bessière. Tel: 05 65 22 14 25.
Open: daily 2–6pm. Free admission.

Musée de Plein-Air du Quercy-Cuzals

This open-air museum spread out over 50 hectares (125 acres) contains a medieval farm, with demonstrations of agricultural and domestic scenes from the time. You can see bread-baking and sheep-shearing, or just enjoy walking around the site. A gentle, highly enjoyable visit.

Domaine de Cuzals, 46330 Sauliac-sur-Célé. Tel: 05 65 31 36 43. Open: Jun–Sept daily 10am–7pm, rest of year Wed–Sun 2–6pm. Admission charge.

Carennac

A lovely small town on the banks of the Dordogne river, but in the Lot region, this was founded in the 11th century around a priory, and still has a beautiful Romanesque church and lovely Gothic cloister. There is also a 16th-century castle where author François Fénelon lived in the mid-17th century. It's classified as one of the 'most beautiful villages in France', along with the neighbouring villages of Loubressac and Turenne. This is also close to the Gouffre de Padirac caves and Rocamadour perched village (*see p106*).

Château de Chambert

To get a feel for the new generation of Cahors wine, but in a property that will be interesting for the whole family, head to this château. A beautiful 13th-century estate where all winemaking is biodynamic, it is part of the Accueil Vigneron programme that promises to welcome visitors and to offer tastings – and all just 35km (22 miles) from Cahors.

Les Hauts Côteaux, 46700 Floressas. Tel: 05 65 31 95 75.
www.chateaudechambert.com.
Open: Mon–Fri 9am–12.30pm & 2–5.30pm, Sat 10am–12.30pm & 3–5.30pm.

Château de Cenevières

Worth the trip for the view alone, this château's terraces offer an amazing panorama over the Lot valley. One of the oldest châteaux in the region, it dates from the 9th century, and although much of the original structure has been altered, there is still a well-preserved square tower from the 13th century. It is also just 35km (22 miles) from Cahors.

46330 Cenevières. Tel: 05 65 31 27 33. www.chateau-cenevieres.com.
Open: summer Mon–Sat 10am–noon & 2–6.30pm, Sun 2–6.30pm; winter by appointment. Admission charge.

Puy-l'Évêque

A very pretty town looking over the river Lot, it has plenty of 13th-century buildings, craft shops and pleasant cafés. There are also some attractive stone steps leading down to the former port, known as La Cale. Vineyards are plentiful here for wine tasting, and there are also a number of canoe hire spots along the river. A market is held in the place de la Mairie central square every Tuesday morning.

Puy-l'Évêque

Drive: Around the bastide towns

The bastide towns are a striking feature of the landscape found across southwest France, many built around 700 years ago during the Hundred Years War. They all have outside walls and the remnants of gates that once formed the only way in and out. Almost all have an arcaded central square where markets have been held for hundreds of years. See map on p103.

This drive covers 100km (62 miles) and should take around four hours, but of course can be easily extended by walks and a long lunch, and would be a very enjoyable way of spending a few days if you decided to stay in one of the bastides overnight.

Starting in Cahors, take the D911 and the D13 for approximately 30km (19 miles).

1 Cazals

Cazals has a large central square, the place Hugues Salel, that holds an excellent market on Saturday mornings. The bastide dates from around 1320 and contains several excellent examples of 17th-century merchant houses, reflecting the status that Cazals once had. There is also a large castle to explore, and a pretty lake.

Take the D660 out of Cazals, then turn left onto the D45, passing through the villages of Les Junies and La Masse. This drive is 19km (12 miles).

2 Castelfranc

A lovely bastide town on the banks of the River Vert. There are plenty of vineyards around here, a charming square and market hall and a beautiful central park, the Jardin des Sens (Garden of the Senses). The 14th-century church is a listed historical monument.

Take the avenue du Colonel Pardès out of Castelfranc towards Prayssac and drive through Puy-l'Évêque (you might want to stop off here also, see p113). Take the D68 for 4km (2½ miles), then the D58 to Montcabrier. This drive is 15km (9¼ miles).

3 Montcabrier

This is one of the best preserved of the bastide towns, with roads laid out in parallel lines around a large central square with medieval arcades. There are vestiges here of the original ramparts and fortified gates.

Take the road to Fumel from the centre of Montcabrier, a lovely route with good views. *At Condat, turn onto the D911 through Tempoure and Cezerac. At Montayral turn left onto the D656, then take the D18 into Montaigu-de-Quercy, following signs for the lake. This drive covers 32km (20 miles).*

4 Lac de Montaigu-de-Quercy

Just over the border into Tarn-et-Garonne, on the border of both the Lot and the Lot-et-Garonne regions, this attractive medieval town sits high on a hilltop. It's a great place to stop for a picnic lunch or a walk, as the lake is one of the largest and most attractive in the area. There are pedalos, boats, canoes and a good sandy beach.
Follow the signs for Auléry out of Montaigu-de-Quercy onto the D953,

then turn quickly left onto the D34 for 4.2km (2½ miles), then get onto the D16 for 3.4km (just over 2 miles), then the D19 passing through Saint-Aureil and into Castelnau-Montratier. This drive is 36km (22 miles).*

5 Castelnau-Montratier

In the 14th century, cloth merchants came here to buy the sought-after wool from the Quercy sheep, and the wealth that was created can still be seen in the handsome architecture of the buildings. Look out for the medieval houses on rue des Orfèvres and the Byzantine-style church.
From here, there is a 45km (28-mile) drive back into Cahors, via the D4 and D653.

Drive: Around the bastide towns

Castelnau-Montratier

LE GERS

Just to the south of the Lot, Le Gers is the heart of the region that is still known as Gascony (although technically, Gascony is an ancient name that refers to large swathes of southwest France). Sitting between Cahors and Toulouse, the fields of Le Gers are full of cereals and sunflowers, punctuated by several handsome market towns. This is the part of France that gave us Dumas' *The Three Musketeers*, and also the well-loved brandy Armagnac. The capital is Auch, which has a beautiful cathedral, some smart shops, and is known as the birthplace of Armagnac. But the soul of the Gers is found in its countryside, and it is most rewarding to visit some of the smaller towns and villages.

Inside Condom's cathedral

Condom

Also known as Condom-en-Armagnac, this smart town is the site of many cultural activities through the summer months, from lively markets to outdoor concerts. In total, 19 sites in Condom are listed as historical monuments by the French government, including its two castles, the cathedral and numerous houses. It also has several links with the international art scene: *Le Bonheur est dans le Pré* (or *Happiness is in the Field*) was filmed here in 1995, and John du Prez, co-composer with Eric Idle of the musical *Spamalot*, has a summer home here.

In terms of getting an overview of the history of Armagnac production in the area, the museum is an excellent place to start (*see opposite*), but nothing is quite as enjoyable as getting out into the surrounding countryside and visiting the many houses that welcome visitors for tours and tastings. The most exciting time for these visits is from October to February, when the distillation is taking place (*www.armagnac.fr*).

Château de Cassaigne

The ancient summer residence of the Bishops of Condom, the château dates from the 13th century (with a 15th-century kitchen still intact), and offers excellent visits in English. It is also a working Armagnac house (traditionally important for the region during periods of conflict, when neighbours' cellars were under threat and they could make good use of its defensive position).

32100 Cassaigne. Tel: 05 62 28 04 02. www.chateaudecassaigne.com. Open: Jun–Sept daily 9am–noon & 2–6pm; rest of the year Tue–Sat 9am–noon & 2–6pm, Sun 9am–noon. Admission charge.

Musée de l'Armagnac

An interesting museum dedicated to France's oldest eau de vie, with records showing its production dating back as far as 1411, its collection is housed in an attractive building that was formerly a bishop's palace. Inside, there are ancient presses and copper stills, and an explanation of the distillation process that is essential for the production of Armagnac.

2 rue Jules Ferry. Tel: 05 62 28 47 17. Open: Apr–Oct Wed–Mon 10am–noon & 3–6pm; rest of the year Wed–Sun 2–5pm. Admission charge.

Fourcès

An essential visit, this very unusual circular bastide is almost impossibly pretty. Originally the houses were built in a circle around a château, but that has since been replaced by a central square filled with plane trees. The whole place is filled with half-timbered houses, spots of greenery, and arcaded streets. A large flower festival is held each April.

Larressingle

This beautifully restored bastide town is reportedly the smallest in France. Just beside the town's ramparts is an interesting – if slightly ramshackle – exhibition of machinery used in the Middle Ages to do everything from producing hydraulic energy to shaping metal into tools and weapons.

Open: throughout the year, but with special events often planned during July and August. Admission charge for the museum.

The fortified walls of Larressingle

Lot-et-Garonne and Les Landes

Here life really slows down to the gentlest of paces. Les Landes comprises 75 per cent forest – almost entirely pine – and 15 per cent agriculture, with just 10 per cent given over to (mainly sleepy) population centres. The Lot-et-Garonne is not far behind, although here agriculture takes centre stage and forests are less prevalent. Between the two regions, industries include papermaking, timber, fruit and vegetable growing and livestock and poultry rearing.

The poultry produced here includes the famous Poulet Jaune of Les Landes, a chicken so named because it is corn-fed and its skin takes on a distinctive yellow colour. The regions are rich with large rivers and lakes, and vast stretches of protected national parkland. All of which makes this part of France absolutely ideal for a laid-back, back-to-nature break.

The main cities include Agen, Marmande, Mont-de-Marsan and Dax. The latter two are far more southern in feel, with plenty of Basque touches evident in the architecture and food. All four of these main population centres have good transport links, but once you are out in the countryside – especially in Les Landes – it is best to hire a car, as public transport can be tricky to come by, with irregular routes and timetables.

The region of Les Landes tracks the Atlantic Coast, so several of its towns and villages are covered in 'The Atlantic Coast' (*see pp60–61*).

LOT-ET-GARONNE

The Lot-et-Garonne forms a lush plain around the wide River Lot, and is proud of its ever-evolving gourmet traditions, from local truffles to rich tomatoes and fragrant strawberries. The most prized fruits of the region are perhaps the plums and prunes of Agen, and vast orchards can be seen around the town. The region's culinary successes have been widely recognised: for such an uninhabited region – there are just 300,000 people living in this beautifully gentle part of the country, with 30,000 in the regional capital of Agen – there are seven Michelin-starred chefs, all producing exciting, innovative cuisine out of these most traditional of ingredients.

Agen

The regional capital of the Lot-et-Garonne is not the most beautiful city in France, but it does contain plenty of treasures for those willing to explore. It contains a number of medieval churches, an impressive cathedral, some attractive medieval streets and a good archaeological museum. You can also walk along the pleasant banks of the Garonne river, or use this as a useful starting point for a boat trip along the Canal du Midi.

Musée des Beaux-Arts (Fine Arts Museum)

One of the largest art museums in southwest France, this is known for its collection of Goya paintings and Palissy ceramics. It's housed in adjoining Renaissance buildings from the 16th and 17th centuries, with a lovely internal courtyard. Inside, permanent and temporary exhibitions display

around 2,000 works of art.
*Place du Docteur Pierre Esquirol.
Tel: 05 53 69 47 23. Open: May–Sept
Wed–Mon 10am–6pm; rest of the year
Wed–Mon 10am–12.30pm & 1–6pm.
Admission charge.*

Buzet-sur-Baïse

One of the largest wine cooperatives in the region, **Les Vignerons de Buzet**, makes for an interesting visit in this pretty village on the River Baïse. There is a large boutique and tasting room, and tours are offered around the facilities.
*Les Vignerons, 47160 Buzet-sur-Baïse.
Tel: 05 53 84 74 30. Email:
buzet@vignerons-buzet.fr.*

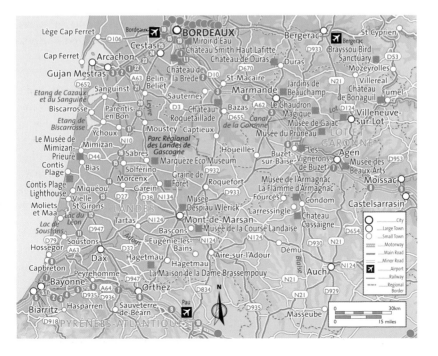

www.vignerons-buzet.fr. Open: Mon–Sat 9am–12.30pm & 2–6pm; later opening times in summer. Free admission. The nearest train station is at Aiguillon 5km (3 miles) away, or a larger station at Tonneins, 15km (9 miles) away.

Duras

The lively market town of Duras, situated where the Lot-et-Garonne approaches the Gironde *département*, is home to the **Château de Duras**, originally constructed in the 13th century but beefed up during the 14th. Inside the castle, there is an attractive Italian-style inner courtyard, a traditional stone breadmaking kitchen

MUSÉE DU PRUNEAU (PRUNE MUSEUM)

The truly emblematic fruit of the Lot-et-Garonne is the prune – the dried plum that has been treasured since the 12th century when the Crusaders brought damson trees back from their Syrian expeditions, and crossed them with a local plum which, when dried in the sun, can be preserved for up to a year. Traditionally, plums were left outdoors on trays of straw and then dried in bread ovens. Today, drying takes place in tunnels with powerful high-temperature ventilation. You will find prunes at roadside stalls throughout the region, but a visit to this museum gives you the chance to taste them at every stage – from fresh plums to dried prunes, and in a variety of gourmet states from chocolate-wrapped to an essential ingredient in the local eau de vie.
Granges-sur-Lot, 47320 Lafitte-sur-Lot. Open: Mon–Sat 9am–noon & 2–7pm, Sun 3–7pm. www.musee-du-pruneau.com. Admission charge.

and numerous well-restored living rooms and galleries.
Château de Duras, place du Château. Tel: 05 53 83 77 32. www.chateau-de-duras.com. Open: Jul–Aug daily 10am–7pm; Apr–Jun & Sept–Oct 10.30am–1pm & 2–7pm; rest of the year 2–6pm. Admission charge. The nearest train station is 24km (15 miles) away in Marmande.

Marmande

Marmande is known, rather unromantically, as the tomato capital of France. It has some pretty features in the town centre, but is certainly on the low-key side. Its **Jardins de Beauchamp**, however, are a real highlight, tucked away in a little-visited part of town behind a garden centre. Don't let any of that put you off – this is a lovely spot. Opened in 2004, it is divided into a Japanese area, an English area, a water garden, a traditional French kitchen garden, and even has a small maze.
Jardins de Beauchamp, rue des Isserts. Tel: 05 53 64 30 12. www.jardineriejay.com. Open: Tue–Sun 9.30am–noon & 2–6.30pm, Mon 2–6.30pm. Admission charge.

Villereal

This is a medieval bastide town that has a fully intact 14th-century market hall in its central square. The best day to visit is Saturday, when a large market sees many of the region's farmers and wine producers converge to sell their

wares. A number of the half-timbered houses around the square, and in the narrow surrounding streets, date from the 16th century.
Villereal tourist office. Tel: 05 53 36 09 65. www.villereal-tourisme.com

Lac du Brayssou

Just outside Villereal, near the village of Tourliac, lies the Lac du Brayssou, a pretty lake (created in 1988) that is also a nature reserve and bird sanctuary. A walk around the entire lake covers 6km (3¾ miles), and you should allow around two or three hours. Birds here include swans, ducks and herons on the lake, but also falcons, buzzards, doves, woodpigeons and many others that

either live here year-round or stop over during migration. An observatory at one of the highest points of the lake points out the species that you are likely to see.
47210 Tourliac. Tel: for walking information 05 53 66 13 33.

Château de Bonaguil

A classified monument near Fumel, this medieval castle is one of the best preserved of the many castles and châteaux of this area, with a large esplanade from the 18th century, and towers and grottoes from the 15th century and earlier. There's a good visitor programme also, as the château hosts various cultural events

Sculpture in the Jardins de Beauchamp, Marmande

Lot-et-Garonne and Les Landes

throughout the year, including a large car rally in September.

47500 Fumel. Tel: 05 53 71 90 33. Email: chateau-bonaguil@wanadoo.fr. www.bonaguil.org. Open: Jul–Aug daily 10am–7pm; rest of the year 10am–noon & 2–6pm. See website for special events. Admission charge.

Le Chaudron Magique

Well worth the drive to get here, this is a working farm in the Lot-et-Garonne that offers visitors the chance to make cheese, milk goats, make bread and generally learn about looking after animals and working the land. There are also demonstrations and workshops in textile weaving and the use of natural dyes to colour the wool that is

CAN THERE REALLY BE A HUMANE *FOIE GRAS* FARM?

This highly divisive topic is hard to ignore in France, particularly in the southwest. Across the country, it is a multimillion-euro industry, employing 30,000 people, and producing 21,000 tonnes of *foie gras* per year (around 75 per cent of the global total). There are some large-scale producers, but sustainable, green approaches to food and farming are part of the lifestyle here, and you can still find traditional *foie gras* farms. At **Ferme Gassiot**, in the village of Cocumont, ducks are given large fields to roam around in, and are hand-fed rather than forced into cages when undergoing the *gavage* (force-feeding). 'It is slower, and you need patience', says the farm's Francis Menville, 'but the ducks are not stressed, and that comes through in the flavours.'
Tel: 05 53 94 50 34.

MESSING ABOUT IN BOATS

With 200km (124 miles) of navigable waterways, the Lot-et-Garonne is the perfect region for getting out onto the water, whether on the Canal de la Garonne, the Lot or (the particularly pretty) Baïse rivers, or the variety of lakes. You generally don't need a permit to hire a boat, and there are plenty of opportunities to take one out for an hour or half a day – or to take a guided cruise on a traditional *gabare*, the flat-bottomed boats once used for the transport of goods and wine up to Bordeaux and beyond. Moor up to explore the Château de Bonaguil in Fumel (*see p121*), the medieval castle at Duras (*see p120*) or the exquisite Pujols-le-Haut, an attractive fortified town near Villeneuve-sur-Lot.
For boat hire suggestions, see p143.

sheared from the several breeds of sheep raised here. It's great for children of course, but interesting for all ages, and you can even spend a week or longer helping out on a farm stay.
47260 Brugnac. Tel: 05 53 88 80 77. www.chaudronmagique.fr. Open: Jun–Aug daily 10am–7pm; Sept–May 3–6pm. Admission charge.

Villeneuve-sur-Lot

This village and area, one of the lushest parts of the region, was known for its market gardens, producing fruits and vegetables that were sought after all over France in the 19th century. Although less wealthy today, this is still a beautiful town to visit, with several interesting museums. The Quai d'Alsace, near Pont Vieux, offers boat trips along the river over the summer months, or you can

take out a slow-gliding electric boat yourself, without a licence.
Tourist office, 3 place de la Libération.
Tel: 05 53 36 17 30.

Musée de Gajac

Housed in a former mill on the banks of the river, this museum contains a large collection of fine paintings, as well as a frequently changing roster of visiting exhibitions, and a good programme of workshops and talks from painters and other artists.
2 rue des Jardins. Tel: 05 53 40 48 00.
Open: Mon–Fri 10am–noon & 2–6pm,
Sat & Sun 2–6pm. Free admission.

Hire a boat on the Canal de Garonne at Buzet-sur-Baïse

Château de Duras

LES LANDES

Although it is sparsely populated for much of the year, thousands of French families have second homes in Les Landes, reflecting the still-powerful connection that the country has with its agricultural roots. The Landes region is banked on one side by the Atlantic Ocean, and many of its coastal resorts are described in the section on 'The Atlantic Coast' (*see pp60–61*). But inland, things slow down pretty dramatically, pretty quickly. This area is best known for its pine forests, which stretch for many kilometres and offer protection from Atlantic winds as well as providing a healthy industry in terms of logging and paper production. As you head to the south of the Landes, the region takes on a more Spanish feel, in the towns of Dax and Aire-sur-l'Adour.

Through the heart of Les Landes flows the lovely River Leyre, which includes some stretches that allow (gentle) white-water rafting. In other parts it is surrounded on both sides by dense bands of trees, making for adventurous navigating that has given it the name 'Little Amazon'. As the river becomes a delta, and flows into the Leyre estuary at the southern tip of the Bassin d'Arcachon (*see pp54–5*), it affords excellent birdwatching opportunities. Some of the best places to join the river for boating or canoeing include Pissos, Sabres and La Teich.

The capital city of the region is Mont-de-Marsan, an elegant town with old merchants' houses dating from the 17th century. Laid-back but with an air of prosperity, Mont-de-Marsan comes alive every July with the Fêtes de la

Madeleine, when the whole town centre is shut off to cars, and thousands of people descend on the area for five days of celebrations.

Aire-sur-l'Adour

One of the oldest towns in the Landes region, this was the site of an important victory for the Romans. As the name suggests, the River Adour dominates the town today and has helped to establish it as an important trading centre over the centuries. For many years, this was known as the regional capital of *foie gras*, and you will still see a lively *foie gras* market and several varieties of duck products for sale in local shops. The large Halle aux Grains was the original marketplace (and then a cinema during the 1930s). This attractive stone building was fully restored in the early 1990s, and is now used for exhibitions and cultural events. This is a small, laid-back town that is best known today for its bullring.

Lac de Léon

This peaceful and beautifully positioned lake is set back from the coastal road in the small town of Léon. The lake is slightly less polished than many of the resorts around here, which makes it all the more charming, because it gets less crowded in high summer and has plenty of shady corners for getting away from it all. There is safe swimming for all ages, a large campsite, various excursions

Decorative letter box, Les Landres

along the Leyre river (*see p124*), and boating opportunities in the form of pedalos, kayaks and windsurfing. *40550 Léon.*

Écomusée de Marquèze (Marquèze Eco Museum)

Worth making a detour for, this open-air museum re-creates the life of peasants and landowners in 18th- and 19th-century Landes. A modern and well-stocked boutique greets you, followed by a contemporary museum that looks at the history and present-day situation of the area, and from there things get progressively old school. To help you step back in time, a century-old train takes you far from the site of the boutique and museum, out on a trundling track to a collection of restored or re-created houses, mills, farms and cottages that you can walk

RESIN TAPPING

By the 19th century, the two main industries in Les Landes were lumber-jacking (which continues today) and resin tapping, where a man cuts into a tree trunk until it 'bleeds' resin, and has to then keep the wound open to ensure a continued supply – an extremely labour-intensive task. The resin is then distilled into turpentine or products used to make soap or paint. The industry, still practised in China, Malaysia and Brazil, dates from the Middle Ages, and in France employed several thousand *résiniers* until the 1960s, when the last commercial factories closed down. The private *résiniers* hung on for another 30 years, but today it is not economically viable and is demonstrated only as a tourist attraction in France.

round, and regular events such as sheep-shearing, breadmaking, harvesting and milking can be seen or participated in. A great restaurant is also on site (best to book ahead in the summer months, or at least when you arrive at the front entrance before you get on the train). *Route de Solferino, 40630 Sabres. Tel: 05 58 08 31 31. www.ecotourisme-landes-de-Gascogne.fr. Admission charge.*

Garein de Forêt

Another open-air museum, in Garein, next door to Sabres, explains forestry, from taking a seed and turning it into first a tree and then a forest. This is the perfect place for learning about this industry, as forestry in this part of France is very much man-made: the pine trees you see all about you in Les Landes were planted only around 150 years ago to try to improve the marshy and unproductive lands that covered this part of France. *Garein. www.grainedeforet.fr. Open: Jul–Aug daily 9.30am–12.30pm & 2–6pm; Apr–Jun & Sept–Oct Sun & public holidays 1–6pm. Admission charge.*

Eugénie-les-Bains

In a region that is rich in places offering thermal cures, this is one of the most famous spas in France. Pretty much everything in this town is geared towards health and rejuvenation, from the large formal park in the centre to the many diet-conscious dishes on restaurant menus.

Tourist office, place Gaston Larrieu.
Tel: 05 58 51 13 16.
www.ville-eugenie-les-bains.fr

Bascons

Fans of the bullfighting that takes place in this lovely town (known as La Course Landaise) are keen to point out that no bulls are ever harmed, and that rather it is almost a dance performed with the great animals, dating from the 15th century. Make up your own mind at the fascinating **Musée de la Course Landaise**, which looks at the history of the sport and how it is practised today, through videos and first-hand oral histories given by its key players.

Musée de la Course Landaise, 40090 Bascons. Tel: 05 58 52 91 76.
Open: Wed–Fri 2.30–6pm, or by appointment. Free admission.

Soustons

This attractive town is divided into two sections: one on the Atlantic Ocean, with several beaches, and the other on a

Lac de Soustons

large freshwater lake, le **Lac de Soustons**. Located around 7km (4¼ miles) from the coast, the lake has a large watersports centre (*www.rowingcentersoustons.com*) that is often used for training Olympic rowers – and also cyclists, who take the track around the outside. *Tourist office. Tel: 05 58 41 52 62. www.soustons.fr. A navette bus runs from Soustons centre to the lake, and to the beaches over the summer months.*

Mont-de-Marsan

The capital of the Landes region, Mont-de-Marsan is a small but vibrant town with a strong cultural scene, and more than a little of the southern feel of Toulouse about it. For the past eight years, every May has seen exhibitions of sculptures throughout the streets of the town, reflecting a strong link with this art form that reaches its full expression in the wonderful **Musée Despiau Wlérick**. The museum specialises in

The *Fontaine Chaude* (hot spring), Dax

figurative sculpture produced between 1880 and 1950. As the name suggests, the majority of the collections centre on two sculptors working between the wars: Charles Despiau and Robert Wlérick, but in total there are over 1,800 sculptures here.

Musée Despiau Wlérick, 6 place Marguerite de Navarre. Tel: 05 58 75 00 45. Open: May–Sept daily 10am–noon & 2–6pm; Oct–Apr Wed–Mon 10am–noon & 2–6pm. Admission charge.

Dax

A leading spa resort in France, Dax lays claim to be the first Roman spa on (what is now) French soil, sourced from a hot spring called La Nehe. Today, the town continues to be a centre for spa-seekers, with around 60,000 visitors per year, and is the site of the National Institute of Thermal Therapy, the largest of its kind in Europe.

CHALOSSE AND TURSAN

A richly beautiful corner of the region, this area marks the meeting point of Les Landes, Béarn and the Gers, just to the north of the Pays Basque. The heart of the region is the Adour river and the town of Aire-sur-l'Adour (*see p125*).

Brassempouy

The main draw here is the very interesting archaeological museum, **La Maison de la Dame de Brassempouy**, opened in 2002, which marks the spot best known for the discovery of the Dame de Brassempouy (the Lady of

La Dame à la Capuche

Brassempouy) or the Dame à la Capuche (Lady with the Hood) in caves just above the village. This large ivory figure is thought to have been carved 25,000 years ago, and although the original is now housed in the Musée d'Archéologie Nationale in Paris, a replica is on show here, along with other artefacts found in the caves, including ancient sculpture and tools. There is also a good boutique, and plenty to explore in the village itself, most notably a large park connected to the museum, and a Roman-style church.

La Maison de la Dame de Brassempouy, 352 rue du Musée. Tel: 05 58 89 21 73. Open: summer daily 2–7pm; winter Tue–Sun 2–6pm. Admission charge.

Walk: Santiago de Compostela

The Santiago de Compostela (Saint-Jacques de Compostelle in French), the most famous pilgrimage route in Europe, threads throughout the southwest of France. Now a popular hiking as well as spiritual route, it offers many opportunities for people wanting to experience shorter sections of this ancient pilgrimage trail, with walks lasting from a few hours to a few weeks.

The original pilgrims who walked the route would have done so around 800 to 1,000 years ago (beginning around AD 950), starting from Vézelay in northeastern France, moving down through France towards the Pyrénées and over into Compostela in Spain. The pilgrims travelled in groups for safety, and many of the villages of the region grew up around their stopping points, where an industry sprang up feeding and housing them along the way. Many of these places continue to offer tourists and walkers a welcome respite today – and even if the pleasures have turned more secular through the centuries, there is still a spiritual experience to be found by getting out and enjoying the great outdoors with just the sound of your feet pounding these ancient pathways.

There are several 'official' routes passing through the Lot-et-Garonne and Landes regions, some that pass down the coast, and others that go through the heart of the interior. One of the best routes to follow is from Onesse-et-Laharie to Lesperon. This walk covers just under 13km (8 miles), and so could be done in theory in one day. This is particularly pretty because you walk through the forest for much of the way. The start of the route is

Waymarker near Mimizan

close to Mimizan, so accessible from a busy tourist centre, but the peace and solitude during the walk make you feel you are far from civilisation.

1 At Onesse, take the D140 south to Lesperon (these really merge into one). Cross the Onesse stream and head up towards the forest, around 1km ($^2/_3$ mile) down the road.

2 At the entrance to the forest, don't stay on the D140, but head up on the grassy path that runs alongside the forest. Follow this path until you arrive at 'Le Grand Coulin' house. This part of the walk covers around 1.6km (1 mile).

3 At Le Grand Coulin, take the dirt track that you see straight ahead of you, and follow this for 2km (1¼ miles), past some lovely pine trees. Whenever you have the option, keep taking the right-hand (west) fork until you eventually meet the road again.

4 Turn left on to the road and stay on it for 1.5km (just under a mile), crossing a valley and the Harencin stream. You will have lovely views of the pine forests at this point.

5 When you reach the top of the valley, you can continue straight along the D140 into Lesperon (4.8km/3 miles away) if you would like to shorten the walk. Alternatively, turn left, onto a dirt track that goes upwards past some ruins. Just after the ruins, take the

grassy path that heads off towards another bank of pine trees, then follow the telephone lines west towards the D140, where you turn left towards Lesperon.

6 There is a quiet beach not far from Lesperon with plenty of watersports facilities. This is a good place to spend the night.

For more information on this route and others, contact Les Amis de Saint Jacques. Tel: 05 58 93 38 33. www.compostelle-landes.com

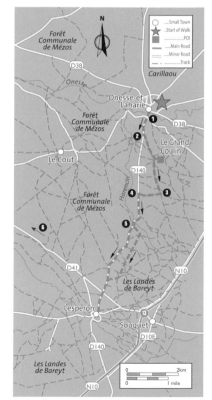

Getting away from it all

There are five regional parks (Les Landes, Causses du Quercy, Grands Causses, Gorges du Tarn and Périgord-Limousin) and one national park (Parc National des Pyrénées) in southwest France, besides the countless kilometres of utterly undisturbed coastline, where you can walk for hours without meeting another person. Throughout the region you will find beauty spots and stretches of open countryside and forest, making this region a real pleasure for those who love the great outdoors.

The three beauty spots below offer a wonderful mix of landscapes, from stunning to gently peaceful, depending on your mood and inclination.

La Réserve Naturelle du Courant d'Huchet, Les Landes

Located within the regional park of Les Landes, the Courant d'Huchet (Huchet

Tree-lined road, Causses du Quercy

Stream) stretches from the Lac de Léon (*see pp125–6*) to the Atlantic Ocean. Although it runs for just 9km (5 miles), it feels like another world, bordered by hibiscus trees, southern oaks and countless species of ferns and other plants and foliage that together form a tunnel of natural vegetation.

The Courant d'Huchet is the only waterway in the Landes that doesn't have a fixed river mouth (despite several attempts to control it), and the changes in the final course of the river into the ocean are carefully adapted to each year by the village of Moliets. The river is a protected site in recognition of its enormous diversity of wild plants and animals. The stream was discovered in 1908 by the Italian poet Gabriele d'Annunzio, and from 1934 was classified as a site of national importance.

Around the Huchet, there is a further 617 hectares (1,525 acres) of a protected nature reserve that has been recognised in its current form since 1981. This nature reserve contains the

The Courant d'Huchet at Moliets

Lac de Léon, large stretches of marshland, the pine-tree covered dunes and the Courant d'Huchet itself.

There are several ways to get to know this area, but all involve going either by boat (and even then, only an approved boat trip organised by the Bateliers du Courant d'Huchet) or by foot. No motorboats are allowed, and neither are dogs, bicycles, horses or cars, all of which maintains the truly peaceful, out-of-time feeling of this place. And day trips only – no camping is allowed.

One of the best places from which to organise trips into the reserve is the Lac de Léon. Here you'll find an attractively rustic Maison de la Réserve information centre that can give you plenty of details about what you will see during your visit, and how best to get there. You can either take a guided walk through the reserve, make your own way by following a map and prescribed footpaths, or by joining an organised boat trip, where you climb into a flat-bottomed boat with around 15 or 20 others, and sit back and relax as you glide through endless green curtains. If you choose to walk, you'll find several viewing stations and bird-watching huts along the way, and signs explaining the history of the reserve and the biodiversity programmes that are in place to keep its natural inhabitants well protected. The organised walks last between two and four hours, and you can choose to follow one deep into the forest, or along the marshes or dunes.

Maison de la Réserve, 374 rue des Bergues du Lac, 40550 Lac de Léon. Tel: 05 58 48 73 91. www.reservenaturelle-couranthuchet.org. Open: Mon–Fri 10am–12.30pm & 2–6pm, Sat 10am–12.30pm & 2.30–6pm, Sun 3–6pm. Train to Moliets-et-Maa station.

Le Chemin des Cascades, Parc National des Pyrénées

The Pyrenean national park covers 100km (62 miles) from east to west, and is packed with hot springs, high peaks, walking trails and wild animals (including endangered brown bears, lynxes and marmots, *see pp86–7*). In total, it covers the six valleys of Aspe, Ossau, Azun, Cauterets, Luz-Gavarnie and Aure. Each has its own distinctive features, from forests in Aspe to the world-famous natural amphitheatres caused by glacial erosion in Luz-Gavarnie (the Cirque de Gavarnie is a UNESCO World Heritage Site, with peaks rising up to 3,000m/9,840ft and containing the tallest waterfall in Europe).

It is nearly impossible to narrow down the best place in this stunning national park for getting away from it

Lush vista in the French Pyrénées

all, as the entire area is criss-crossed with hiking trails around forests, lakes, rivers, cliff tops and every other feasible type of mountain landscape. But one of the unmissable attractions, easily accessible from Lourdes, is the Chemin des Cascades, a walk that passes six large waterfalls and has the added benefit of being attainable in half a day there and back.

To get to the beginning of the walk, take a shuttle bus from the town of Cauterets, or follow a path from the tourist office up past Les Thermes des Griffons (Griffons Thermal Spa), and take the mountain road up to the starting point.

The walk takes you to the Pont d'Espagne (Spanish Bridge), a brick-built bridge that spans a stunning mountain ravine called the Gave du Marcadau. You will walk up to 1,500m (4,920ft) above sea level at the highest point, but nothing along the walk itself is too strenuous – the route is well shaded for much of the way, and not especially steep. Instead, you'll have plenty of opportunity to drink in the peaceful view as the path follows along the Jéret valley and its many waterfalls. The first waterfall you will get to is the Cascade de Mauhourat, followed by the Escane-Gat, then the Cascade du Ceriset, the Cascade de Pouey Bacooi (particularly stunning, as it flows down through steep rocks), the Cascade du Pas de l'Ours (next to a bridge of the same name), and finally the Cascade de Bousses appears just after the Sarah

Cascade du Lutour

Bernhardt Island. There's a restaurant, hotel and café once you make it to the bridge, and you can easily return by the same route (or, if you want to cheat, a road leads back down to Cauterets from the Pont d'Espagne). You can also take a cable car from here up to the peak of the Vignemale mountain.

A good map of this walk, and others in the area, can be found at the **Maison du Parc** in Cauterets (currently undergoing renovations, but due to be reopened in summer 2011; the Cauterets tourist office (*place du Maréchal Foch. Tel: 05 62 92 50 50*) is the information point in the meantime).

Remember, as when undertaking any mountain walk, to let somebody know the route you are taking, and ensure you are properly equipped for sudden changes in the weather.

Lac de Gaube, near Cauterets

Maison du Parc, place de la Gare, 65110 Cauterets. Tel: 05 62 92 52 56. www.parc-pyrenees.com. A shuttle bus takes you out to the park from Bordenave Excursions (Tel: 05 62 92 53 68).

Sentier d'Argentine, Parc Naturel Périgord-Limousin

This newly created regional park (established in 1998) covers over 1,800sq km (695sq miles) in the northern regions of the Dordogne, extending northwards into the Haute-Vienne (in the Limousin region) and the foothills of the Massif Central mountains. It is a rolling landscape, punctuated by chestnut forests, limestone escarpments and several meticulously maintained towns and villages. The largest towns of note are Saint-Junien, Aixe-sur-Vienne, Nexon,

Saint-Yrieix-la-Perche, Thiviers and Brantôme, but it is agriculture and animal rearing that take centre stage: on walks you will see small stone huts used for drying out chestnuts, and others used as shelter by shepherds or farmers.

There are over 2,000km (1,240 miles) of walking and cycling routes all over the park, some of which are completely untouched, while others have been punctuated with information boards and signs explaining the area and its wildlife. Swimming and fishing are possible in the many lakes and rivers. This is also the stage for numerous intensive ecological projects aimed at protecting the natural landscape and its biodiversity. From 2006, one of these initiatives has been to develop certified products of the Périgord-Limousin park, launched first with a local honey, then followed by chestnut jams and goat's cheese. There are also projects to encourage ecotourism initiatives that help visitors to sustain the park rather than damaging it.

A particularly peaceful walk is tucked into the southwestern corner of the park, near the town of Mareuil in the Périgord valley. Known as the Sentier d'Argentine, this walking path (or paths, as there are several trails) follows the Argentine limestone escarpment, an area of outstanding natural beauty. You are at the meeting of the Nizonne, Charente and Dordogne rivers here also, affording plenty of other quiet strolls along the riverbanks. If you head onto the escarpment rather than to the river, you will find several walking paths that loop around the entire Plateau d'Argentine, covering in total 5km (3 miles) of tracks that have clearly marked signs describing the flora and fauna of the area, and its evolving landscape.

The Sentier d'Argentine starts at the tiny village of Argentine, where today you will find just three or four houses (for provisions, the neighbouring town of La Rochebeaucourt is a better bet), along with an 11th-century church and the remains of an old Roman road. There are also the ruins – little more than a few walls and a well – of a castle.

Leaving this behind, the walk passes through, among other things, a mushroom quarry that is particularly attractive in autumn, and rare orchids that bloom in between the limestone rocks during spring. You can also explore three local caves – La Grotte des Anglais, La Grotte des Tombeaux and the Grotte de l'Église – which were used by the English to shelter during the Hundred Years War, and by the Maquis Resistance (rural guerrilla groups) during World War II.
Syndicat d'Initiative de Mareuil.
Tel: 05 53 60 99 85. www.parc-naturel-perigord-limousin.fr. There is a car park at the start of the trail.

Shepherds' hut, Périgord-Limousin

When to go

With its mix of large cities, beaches, mountains and gourmet pleasures, there's something to see and do in southwest France throughout the year, giving you plenty of flexibility when deciding on dates for your trip. The southwest of the country does not enjoy quite the same uninterrupted sunshine as the southeast of France and the Côte d'Azur, but it still has a largely stable and clement climate, becoming warmer and sunnier the closer you get to the Spanish border.

Weather is thus not a particularly major concern, and you might instead want to base your holiday dates on times of the year that offer the best chance of avoiding queues both on the motorways and at major attractions. As with much of France, things get very busy from mid-July to mid-August, when the whole of the country takes its *grandes vacances* (summer school holidays). If you are planning to travel by car any time between 14 July and 14 August, always check travel updates before you go, and try to travel late at night or early in the morning: the worst days are signified 'Red' on the roads, and can involve sitting bumper to bumper for hours.

The best times of year for both good weather and crowd avoidance are May–June and September–October. If you are planning to ski, the season starts a little later and finishes a little earlier than in the Alps, as the mountains in the southwest are not quite as high. Expect the usual

season to last from late December to early April.

For wine lovers, harvest (falling in September and October in most years) is fascinating, and most estates are now open for visitors during this busy time, so you can enjoy the novel experience

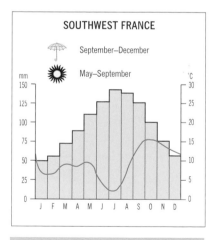

WEATHER CONVERSION
CHART

25.4mm = 1 inch
°F = 1.8 × °C + 32

The *vendange* (grape harvest) falls in early autumn

of drinking *vin bourru* – a young wine in its very early stages. Surfers are usually attracted to the region during the summer months, when numerous festivals and competitions take place up and down the coast. Food lovers are attracted by the mountains of fresh produce to be found in markets over the summer and autumn months, but remember that there are plenty of regional specialities in every season – truffle lovers, for example, should be booking their tickets for January and February.

Weather-wise, springtime begins usually in March or April, with temperatures climbing from the early teens up to an average of 20°C (68°F). Things can get very hot in summer, with a July and August average of 28°C (82°F) and over ten hours of sunshine a day. It can rain a lot in autumn (often up to 200mm/8in per month in September and October), but things are still warm at this time of year, with an average of 23°C (74°F). Snow has been known in winter, but it's rarely freezing.

Getting around

Southwest France has several major motorways, airports of various sizes, numerous train stations and a good bus, tram and coach network (although the frequency of these is directly proportional to the size of the town or village that they serve), so exploring the region shouldn't be a problem in theory. In practice, however, most people who live here – and particularly those who live in the countryside – continue to rely heavily on cars.

By train

If you are planning to visit just the major cities (and a fair few of the towns), the train network will do the job. The super-fast and aptly named **TGV** (Train à Grande Vitesse, or High-speed Train) network runs from Paris to the big cities – most frequently to Bordeaux and Toulouse, but also to Saint-Jean-de-Luz, Biarritz, Pau, Bayonne, Agen and a number of other cities (*www.tgv.com*). Journey time from Paris to Bordeaux is three hours, although this should shorten over the next few years. Once you have reached these bigger cities, the local train services will take over, run by Corail for the Midi-Pyrénées and by **TER Aquitaine** for elsewhere (*www.ter-sncf.com/aquitaine*). These have both old and new stock running on the lines, and if you're lucky you'll catch one of the newer trains. There are a number of tourist trains running in the mountains and in the Dordogne, but most local trains are slow and fairly irregular.

On the plus side, they are fairly inexpensive, and most tickets can be changed very easily up to the time of travel.

If you do plan to make use of the rail network, consider buying a travel pass. Across France there are special tickets on offer for families, and it often works out cheaper to travel with two or more children than on your own! Check at any railway station for current offers. Also bear in mind that many train stations, particularly local ones, do not have great access for those with mobility issues.

By bus

Buses do travel to some places that local trains do not, but by and large, in the rural parts of southwest France neither buses nor trains are particularly brilliant and you will have to carefully plan ahead to ensure you catch the infrequent services. In the main cities, it is a different story and you will find it very easy to navigate around the bus system. In Bordeaux, it is worth knowing that recent years have seen the introduction of a bus service, aimed at students, for visiting the vineyards. It's called **Bordeaux Bus** and runs through the summer months (ask at any tourist office for details). For buses across the Pays Basque region, a useful website (although only in French) is *www.transdev-atcrb.com*. Links to other bus services across the region can be found at *www.transbus.org*. Remember also that many of these destinations rely on tourists, and so buses are laid on over the summer months, ensuring that happy visitors arrive at the right destinations. To this end, you can take buses throughout the summer months from central Bordeaux right out to the beaches of Arcachon and the Atlantic Coast, and similar tourist buses run from Saint-Jean-de-Luz and Biarritz up into the Pyrénées.

By tram or metro
Public transport around the region's two biggest cities is not confined just to buses. Bordeaux has a highly efficient and modern tram system (*see below*), while Toulouse has its own equally efficient metro service. Both are fairly simple: Bordeaux has three tram lines (a fourth, Line D, is planned but not yet finalised), while Toulouse has two

Bordeaux tramway

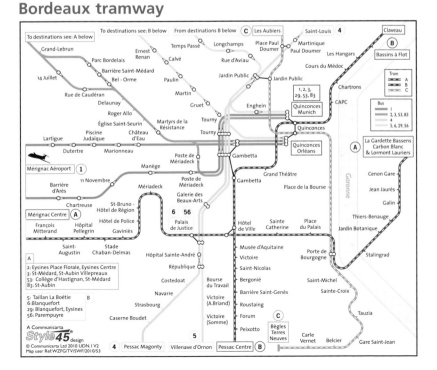

Road train, Lourdes

metro lines, one going east-west (Line A) and one going north-south (Line B). Bordeaux's trams are that much more attractive than Toulouse's metro because they remain above ground, and so you don't miss any of the sights while you are travelling about, but both systems are inexpensive, clean and safe ways to travel around the cities. There is excellent disabled access on both systems – particularly the Bordeaux trams.

By car

If you are planning to tour around southwest France, it is hard to beat the car for convenience, and this is also beautiful driving country, particularly around the stunning mountain roads in the Pyrénées or the cliff-top drives alongside gorges in the Dordogne.

Once you head into these smaller areas, it is very difficult to get effective public transport, so cars are often the sole option available. There are car hire firms at all major airports and train stations, and good motorway links from northern France if you are driving from further afield or bringing your own car from the UK. Generally speaking, motorways and smaller roads tend to be faster-moving than their UK counterparts, simply because France has roughly the same population as the UK but spread out over twice as much space. Distances may therefore be further but actual journey times faster.

The maximum speed limit on most motorways is 130km/h, while on dual carriageways and some country roads it is 90km/h. In towns it drops to 50km/h (and usually 30km/h near schools).

Remember that when driving in France you need your full driving licence and your car's registration certificate on you at all times. An International Driving Licence is necessary for any visitors staying longer than 90 days, otherwise your normal licence is fine. Remember also that the French like to drive fast – and the more narrow and winding the country road, the faster they seem to like it, so be careful. On French motorways, also remember that the outside (fast) lane is for overtaking, and you should spend most of your time in the slower lane. It is a legal requirement for all cars to carry a warning triangle and a reflective safety jacket in case of breakdown.

And, probably most importantly, note that in France cars drive on the right.

By taxi

Taxis are also easily available in the cities of southwest France, although they are few and far between in the country and need to be booked well in advance. Across France, most taxis are required to return to the rank to pick up customers and cannot be flagged down on the street. Unlike in Paris, fares in the southwest are not especially cheap, and prices can add up quickly if you have extra bags. As a rule, a tip of around 10–15 per cent of the fare is appreciated.

By boat

With a little planning, it is perfectly possible to travel through large parts of southwest France by boat. There are navigable canals and rivers, as well as cross-Channel ferries that travel between the UK and the Atlantic sea-ports (the closest to this part of France is probably Saint-Malo). You can also choose to take a cruise down the Atlantic Coast. Among the many companies offering these trips, **French Boat Holidays** has a good range of options (*www.frenchboatholidays.com*).

Boating along the Lot

Accommodation

You can find something to suit every budget here, from glamorous hotels and ski lodges to home-stay chambres d'hôtes, and low-cost campsites. On the whole, accommodation tends to be most plentiful in the cities and along the coast, where large numbers of tourists flock each year. Inevitably your options are more limited in the smaller villages, but some of the best experiences here are to be found on farms that offer home-stay options.

There are also lots of self-catering *gîtes* (holiday cottages, many of which were opened up by Brits starting out a new life in France). Cheaper options, besides camping, include youth hostels (again, most commonly found in cities and in tourist spots such as the beaches and the Pyrénées).

Chambres d'hôtes and gîtes

These two styles of accommodation are enormously popular in France. The main difference between the two (sometimes even offered by the same person but in different parts of their property) is that with a *chambre d'hôte* you are being invited effectively into somebody's home, and you will receive breakfast, and sometimes an evening meal if you book ahead (when more meals than just breakfast are offered, the name changes to a *table d'hôte*). A *chambre d'hôte* by law is not allowed to have more than five bedrooms, so you can be assured of an intimate stay without large numbers of other guests.

A *gîte*, on the other hand, is usually a self-contained apartment or separate holiday cottage, where all catering is done by you, and you are very much left to your own devices. A *gîte* will have its own reception area, bedrooms, kitchen and bathrooms – and by choosing a 'rural *gîte*' (an official classification), you can make sure your holiday takes place in the countryside, in the mountains or by the sea. The property should be well stocked with cooking equipment, cutlery and corkscrews (essential in this part of France!), as well as bedding.
A few useful websites include:
www.gites-de-france.com
www.chambres-hotes-france.org
www.chambresdhotesfrance.com

Camping

There are hundreds of campsites around southwest France, thanks to its beautiful countryside, its many kilometres of beaches and its status (perhaps not entirely disconnected

Hotels along the Gave de Pau, Lourdes

from the first two reasons) as a major tourist destination.

Campsites are given a rating from one to four stars, which tells you about their facilities, from on-site restaurants to swimming pools and hot showers. Price, of course, varies depending on the stars, as well as on the campsite's location. All star levels must provide showers, toilets and wash areas, but after that facilities do differ quite a bit. Along the Atlantic Coast, many of the four-star campsites now have gourmet restaurants and good boutiques selling fine wine and an array of regional produce. And increasing numbers of campsites are offering more unusual accommodation options, such as yurts or teepees.

Another possibility is Camping à la Ferme (Camping at the Farm), where you can combine being outside with experiencing life on a working farm. For this, farmers are allowed to offer a maximum of six pitches, and they must provide toilets, wash basins and at least one hot shower.

Note that in southwest France, particularly along the northern Gironde beaches, there are a number of naturist campsites, so do check carefully before you book anything!

For all of the above, local tourist offices are great sources of information about what is on offer in your chosen area, or try *www.bienvenue-a-la-ferme.com*

Towns such as Sarlat weren't designed for cars

Hiking and skiing accommodation

Once you are up in the mountains of the Pyrénées, whether in summer or winter, there are a number of options. Hikers will find numerous low-cost hotels and *chambres d'hôtes*, and as you head into rougher terrain, there are several mountain huts or refuges that offer a very basic but usually clean and certainly low-cost bed for the night – at the very least, this prevents you from having to lug camping equipment around with you while you hike. Some places will even provide a picnic lunch for you to take the next day! For lists of all the hotel and hut options, contact the local tourist office before setting out on any hikes.

For skiers, many of the same hotels that offer summer hiking stops double as ski chalets in the winter months. All of the big ski resorts, clustered around Andorra but dotted throughout the Pyrénées, have large hotels that offer ski-hire directly, and some of them look straight out over the slopes. The following websites can be useful resources:

www.ffcam.fr
www.clubalpin.com/fr/presrefuge.html
www.pyreneesaccommodation.com
www.pyreneesguide.com

Hotels

Although the hotels in the southwest don't often reach the marble-lined luxury of hotels in Paris or on the Côte d'Azur, it is getting increasingly easy to find seriously upmarket hotels in this part of France, with wonderful service and fantastic views. You can easily part with €200 or more per night at these kinds of places, but the majority of hotel bedrooms start at around €50. (Accommodation prices have definitely gone up in recent years – or at least have started to seem more expensive as the euro strengthens.) Always check if breakfast is included in the room rate, as this is not standard in France, and remember that a small tax will be added on to your bill. If you need any special requirements for access, make sure you specify at the time of booking, as many of the smaller hotels will need to offer you ground-floor rooms because they do not have lifts up to higher floors. In towns and cities, ensure also that you ask about their parking facilities before you arrive, as busy but fairly small towns such as Sarlat can be very challenging for parking.

For suggestions, try *www.innsoffrance.com*

Tree-top accommodation

Increasingly, ecotourism options are springing up around this area. One of the most interesting possibilities on offer is to head up into the trees and spend the night in a (sometimes very glamorous) tree-house. You can currently do this in a Médoc vineyard or in a Dordogne château (*see 'Directory', p175 and pp186–7*).

Food and drink

You're going to need those wide-open spaces of the southwest if you are to have any hope of working off the pleasures of the regional delicacies. There are few corners of France where the locals don't like to eat, and the southwest is no exception. And when you go home, you're going to want to leave with a few items tucked into your suitcase – another excellent reason to choose to drive around the region: car boot space!

Local specialities

Among the treasures of the region are the *caviar d'Aquitaine* (a farmed caviar made in the Bordeaux region), white asparagus from Blaye, tiny spicy peppers from Espelette in the Pyrénées (*see p75*), a dried ham from Bayonne (*see pp16–17*), *foie gras* from the Lot and Lot-et-Garonne, and countless regional cheeses and pâtés. Despite the proximity of the Atlantic Ocean, this is a real meat-eating area, with the ubiquitous duck, and wonderful beef from Bazas near Bordeaux and from the Limousin as you head into Périgord. Fish lovers will also have the choice of river fish and ocean catches, and plenty of shellfish, especially around Saint-Jean-de-Luz and the Bassin d'Arcachon.

Great care is taken over food here – even the *gabure*, a local peasant vegetable and cabbage soup, is delicious, and many local restaurants will have a large pot from which you can refill as often as you like. Sweet treats include macaroons from Saint-Émilion (an almond, egg-white and sugar confection), *gâteau Basque* in the Pyrénées and chocolate in Bayonne.

Marché Cristal, Toulouse

The region's most famous dish – cassoulet

Markets

Markets are held around the region pretty much every day of the year. Some of the biggest are Capucins in Bordeaux (every day but Sunday), the riverfront of La Réole in southern Entre-deux-Mers (every Saturday morning), the bastide of Créon, also in Entre-deux-Mers (Wednesday mornings), the Saint-Aubin market in Toulouse (a farmers' market held every Sunday morning), Foix in the Midi-Pyrénées (Friday mornings) and Condom in the Gers (on Wednesday mornings in place Voltaire). But no matter what the day, you will find that one of your local villages will have set up stalls to sell local produce – just ask the tourist office for the list of markets

in whatever area you are staying. To make the most of them while there, take a *panier* (basket), get there early and prepare to enjoy the beautiful displays of regional and seasonal produce. Some companies even offer to accompany you, and then help you cook a meal afterwards with the produce you have secured. Check out *www.twobordelais.com* or *www.theinternationalkitchen.com*

Drinks

As any drive through the countryside here will show you, there are plenty of grapes grown in southwest France. These are put to good use not only in making red, white and rosé wines, but also Armagnac, Cognac (if you head

Wine-based topiary, Bordeaux

just a touch further north) and some good fruit eau de vie. Besides wine, there is some very good cider around the Pays Basque – and plenty of wonderful fresh apple juice also!
For further information, see pp50–51.

Eating out

The residents of the southwest like to eat their local food, and you will find daily *prix fixe* menus in most roadside restaurants that serve up plentiful regional produce at a very reasonable price. As with much of France, meal times are fairly rigid, particularly outside the big cities, and you should expect to be sitting down to eat between noon and 2pm for lunch, and then from 7pm to 10pm for dinner. It is always best to book ahead – small

restaurants in particular will be planning their menus carefully and buying from the local markets, so it helps them to get the best of the produce if you let them know you are coming. And always let them know ahead of time if you have special requests, particularly if you are vegetarian or coeliac: the French do not always cater well for special dietary requirements, and this is particularly so in the southwest, where duck and steak are such major components of most menus. Vegetarians will have no problem eating in the larger cities, and this region grows some wonderful fruit and vegetables, but unless you warn restaurants in advance, you may be faced with an unexciting plate. But don't forget that a fresh truffle omelette

MENUS

A menu in a typical restaurant will be *prix fixe* (fixed price) and will offer the choice of either all three courses (*entrée-plat-dessert*) or a choice of two (either *entrée-plat* or *plat-dessert*). Classic dishes that you will see in southwest France include:

Entrecôte – steak (Entrecote à la bordelaise is a steak cooked in shallots and red wine)

Poulet Basque – Basque-style chicken

Cassoulet – a bean and sausage stew most popular around Toulouse

Confit de canard – duck that has been cooked and preserved in its own fat

Chèvre tiède – warm goat's cheese

Steak-frites – steak and chips

Bouillabaisse – fish soup with pieces of fish

Piperade Basque – omelette stirred into cooked tomatoes, onions and peppers

---

is entirely vegetarian and one of the world's great gourmet delights!

Also remember that smoking is no longer permitted inside restaurants in France. This does have the drawback that it is now only allowed on terraces, so the enjoyment of a summery lunch outside can be somewhat spoiled by the crowds of smokers who congregate outdoors.

Tipping

This can be a confusing subject in France, but generally the first step is to carefully read the bill that you are given. 'Service compris' means service is included, and you should take that at face value. Serving staff in France often see it as a long-term career, not as a way to make extra money while studying or taking time out, as is often the case elsewhere, and they receive full health and pension benefits with their salaries. A service charge of 10 or 15 per cent will have been added to the bill and will later be distributed to them. Other places will say 'Service non compris', and here you are expected to leave around 10 to 15 per cent, but these cases are fairly rare.

Cost

Although there are numerous local restaurants that offer excellent low-cost food (often easily recognised by the number of large trucks parked up outside them at lunchtime), prices in restaurants are not as cheap as they once were in France. A typical three-course meal at lunchtime in a local restaurant will be around €15. Prices rise in the evenings, and in cities.

The Château Montus cellars

Entertainment

There are countless opportunities for entertainment in southwest France, with the format depending largely on where you are. Big cities such as Toulouse, Bordeaux and Biarritz stage large international concerts, ballets, theatre and exhibitions, whereas in the smaller towns and villages you are more likely to experience local festivals, dances and celebrations, and get a real flavour of the very specific culture that is found here.

It's easy to discover what is going on. Make use of the local paper (the *Sud Ouest* covers this whole region and is widely available in newsagents, known as *tabacs*), and there are specialist 'what's on?' guides for the big cities (look out for *Spirit* in Bordeaux, or websites such as *www.toulouseweekend.com* for Toulouse). Almost all venues now have their own website, and often you can book tickets directly. Hotels will almost always have leaflets advertising local events, as will tourist offices, and most regions publish their own 'what's on?' guides (especially during the summer months), which are distributed to railway stations and airports as well as restaurants and hotels.

For the locals, eating out takes precedence over everything else, and plenty of entertainment can be had from a simple early-evening stroll around town followed later by a relaxed dining experience,

especially in places such as Saint-Jean-de-Luz and Biarritz, where the summer evenings are so warm and welcoming.

Festa Tolosa, Toulouse

Festive bands are a feature of summer in the southwest

Tourist attractions

The big sights in the southwest include the Lascaux caves (*see pp108–9*), Château de Bonaguil (*see pp121–2*), Millau suspension bridge (*see pp98–9*) and the Bordeaux vineyards (*see pp28–51*), but there are countless lesser-known attractions that you will either stumble across or be guided towards, such as the Écomusée de Marquèze (*see p126*), or the Musée de l'Art du Sucre (*see pp97–8*), which are wonderful examples of why this area is so richly rewarding to visit. The southwest revels in its status as being a hidden corner of France, and many museums and galleries will celebrate one specific aspect of the local area, whether a traditional industry that supported its growth or an historical figure who lived there.

Cinema

The biggest cities in the southwest usually house several cinemas showing a mix of English-language and French films, and almost all small towns will have at least one screen. Increasingly, you can also find open-air film screenings over the summer months. It is fairly difficult to find VO (*version originale*, or English, in the case of Hollywood blockbusters) screenings, as the French continue to prefer to watch their films dubbed rather than subtitled, and there is a huge industry around dubbing, with many of the voice-over stars being big celebrities in their own right. To find an English-language screening, head to the bigger cities.

Festivals

These are held throughout the year, but most frequently over the summer months, and are a wonderful way to join in with local traditional entertainments. The content of the festivals varies enormously depending on location. Often colourful dancing and competitive sports events take place in the Pays Basque, while in Périgueux and the Dordogne, festivals are often connected to food, and in Toulouse they are about music and contemporary culture… but there are no hard and fast rules. The biggest festivals, such as the Bordeaux Fête le Vin (*see p20*), are worth basing your holiday around.

Live music

This takes several forms, from visiting international musicians to impromptu evenings at local restaurants. In the wine regions, classical concerts are

Inside the Augustins museum, Bordeaux

often held in châteaux, with a tasting after the music – an utterly civilised way to get your music fix. For more contemporary music, large outdoor music festivals have sprung up in recent years – for example, check out the **Reggae Sun Ska Festival**, held in July at a variety of venues around Bordeaux (*www.reggaesunska.com*). The **Jazz in Marciac** festival, every August, is one of the highlights of the musical year across Europe and should not be missed by any music lover (*see p21*). Generally speaking, the larger the student population of a city, the more live music you are going to come across.

Museums

The locals love to celebrate and honour the traditions of the southwest, as may be clearly seen in the impressive array of museums, covering as quirky and varied subjects as the prunes of Agen, the Basque way of life in Saint-Jean-de-Luz, old winemaking instruments in Pauillac, the life and art of Toulouse-Lautrec in Albi, and contraceptive devices in Condom. Many of these are meticulously researched and maintained, even in the smallest of villages, and form a rich part of the entertainment experience in this corner of France.

Sea

Jacques Cousteau, the world-famous marine biologist, was born in Saint-André-de-Cubzac, just to the east of Bordeaux, and began his love for the

FESTIVAL SHAKESPEARE DE QUERCY

A brilliant initiative that was started in 2001 and is held every August is this celebration of the works of William Shakespeare, performed in English in picturesque settings around the Lot valley. The plays (acted by a theatre company that is based in England during the winter months) are usually 'staged' on cobbled streets and village squares – so it might be Monflanquin one night, Puy-l'Évêque the next, and Cahors the next. They have also started to branch out into celebrations of other famous English playwrights: 2010 saw the works of Oscar Wilde performed. On a warm summer evening, these performances can be quite magical, and this is far from tourist fare – plenty of French locals come along to enjoy the spectacle. *www.festivalshakespeare.org*

sea along the Atlantic Coast before heading off to join the navy. The sea remains an essential part of the culture of southwest France, and certainly a key part of the entertainment offered here is through boat trips, cruises, surfing competitions and marine-related activities such as aquariums and water parks.

Theatre

Most of the larger towns in the southwest have at least one theatre, and sometimes three or four. Bordeaux's Grand Théâtre (also an opera house) is one of the few in France to have a permanent ballet and opera company employed by the city itself, rather than welcoming visiting theatre companies on tour (although these do perform here also).

Shopping

Outside of Bordeaux and Toulouse (and, of course, Andorra), this is not a part of France given over to consumerism and high-octane shopping experiences – at least not for international clothes, jewellery and brands. The objects that you will want to take home with you are more likely to be food- and drink-related, or examples of local craftsmanship. The region's plentiful farms offer up a variety of take-home goods, often presented beautifully.

In the Pyrénées, load up on brébis cheese, Espelette peppers, *charcuterie* products and *gâteau Basque* – not forgetting of course a few bottles of Irouléguy wine or local pear eau de vie. Over in the Dordogne or the Lot valley, if you can't afford a whole truffle, look out for truffle-infused olive oil, or find

Wine shop, Saint-Émilion

it laced into butter, pasta or bread. In Bordeaux, the speciality sweet treat is called *canelé*, a special dome-shaped cake (tiny enough to eat in one mouthful) that is crunchy and caramelised on the outside with a deliciously custard-soft interior. You'll also see signs for honey producers, *foie gras* farms, cheese makers and many other local products while you are out driving around, all of which make great purchases and much-appreciated gifts back home. Try to stop off at such places wherever possible, but be aware that most locals will be eating between noon and 2pm and may not appreciate the interruption at this time. If food shopping in more traditional stores, do remember that for environmental reasons many supermarkets no longer provide plastic bags, so be prepared to either pay a small amount for one (ask for *un sac*), or take one along yourself.

Besides the food and wine, there are opportunities to spend some serious money if you have the desire to do so.

Andorra is of course famous for its tax-free shopping status. The Triangle d'Or in Bordeaux is the place for the most chic shops – try **La Galerie des Grands Hommes** (*www.lesgrandshommes.com*) or any of the shops along the beautiful cours de l'Intendance. In Toulouse, the shopping is centred around the place du Capitole and rue de Saint-Rome, but look out for the individual boutiques selling one-off clothes and quirky interior-design items around the rue du Taur and rue de la Pomme.

Antiques are also big in this part of France. There is an annual antiques fair held in Bordeaux's Bordeaux-Lac quarter, and the Chartrons area of the city is absolutely full of antique dealers. The Dordogne is also a great region for antique hunting, particularly at the *brocante* (bric-a-brac/second-hand) markets that seem to be held every Sunday in villages and towns around the area. Book collectors will also enjoy rummaging at the many antique book festivals that are held in the southwest, particularly in Périgueux, Bordeaux and Toulouse. Look out for English-language books, as you can sometimes discover rare titles at wonderful prices, because most of the people buying and browsing are after French-language books. Also in Périgueux, don't miss the opportunity to stroll along the extremely attractive rue Limogeanne, which runs from cours Tourny to place du Coderc and the covered market. This is a pretty, pedestrianised little street lined with stone buildings housing a collection of beautiful shops.

Art sale on the Garonne *berges*, Toulouse

Sport and leisure

With many kilometres of coastline, cycle paths, lakes and green spaces, not to mention a healthy obsession with rugby in most towns you'll stop at, you'll find it hard to remain inactive on a holiday in southwest France. If you just want to really wind down and enjoy a bit of pampering, however, all you need to do is head for one of the numerous thermal spas (see pp76–7) and luxuriate your way to relaxation.

The best way to approach the overwhelming number of options is to decide on the kind of activity you like and then choose your location accordingly. Whatever you end up doing, make sure you're always properly equipped: this should include checking that your health and travel insurance covers you if you undertake any extreme-sport or even general sporting activity.

Walking and hiking

Hiking enthusiasts will want to head either to the Dordogne and the Lot, or down to the Pyrénées mountains, where there are numerous official and unofficial walking routes. For the truly hardy (and those with plenty of leisure time) a coast-to-coast walk from the Atlantic to the Mediterranean is possible along the GR10 hiking trail, which runs from Hendaye to Banyuls-sur-Mer through the mountains, and takes around two months of walking eight hours a day to complete. If you prefer a more level walk, you might

want to join part of the Santiago de Compostela route, which heads right up into the mountains but also passes through more gentle sections of the Gironde and the Lot-et-Garonne. All of the national and regional parks in the area are also full of well-marked – or totally wild, depending on your preference – walking and hiking trails.

The region has numerous golf courses

Rafting on the Gave d'Oloron in the Pyrénées

You'll need to equip yourself with good walking boots, a sunhat and sunblock, and plenty of water before setting out.

A good website to consult before going anywhere is *www.lespyrenees.net*, as it contains a variety of maps and links to professional guiding organisations. Or try the **Fédération Française de la Randonnée Pédestre** (*www.ffrandonnee.fr*), a useful national resource for walking in France, with regional links for the Pyrénées.

Swimming, sailing and watersports

The plethora of rivers and lakes, and kilometres of coastline makes this a paradise for those who love to get out on the water – or for the inexperienced who are willing to take the plunge or just get their feet wet. Swimming is possible in lakes and in the sea, but there are also plenty of water parks and swimming pools. The **Piscine d'Été** (Summer Pool) in Toulouse is particularly attractive, comprising an impressive complex of swimming pools, varying in size, situated on the Île du Ramier right in the centre of town. Outside the main cities, big water parks such as **Aqualand** on the southern side of the Bassin d'Arcachon (*www.aqualand.fr*) offer plenty of splashing opportunities for little ones. All of the beach resorts such as Mimizan or Biarritz have watersports centres where you can hire equipment and organise training.

As a general rule, if you are an experienced sailor or windsurfer, head to the coast, and if you are just beginning, think about the inland lakes, such as Léon in the Lot-et-Garonne (*see pp125–6*), Hourtin in the

Gironde (*www.hourtin-medoc.com*) or Groléjac in the Dordogne (*www.grolejac.com*). You can also go scuba diving either along the coast or in the bay of Arcachon, and you can canoe down the Dordogne. For sailing centres, contact the **Fédération Française de Voile** (*www.ffvoile.org*). More unusual watersports such as kite-surfing are also taking off here (no pun intended…), so it's always a good idea to check with local tourist offices to find out the latest possibilities.

Surfing

This sport is such a big deal here that it deserves its own section. Southwest France has the warm climate of course, but also, more importantly, the waves from the Atlantic Ocean, making this one of the best surfing locations in Europe, and certainly in France. This is still the Atlantic Ocean though, so remember that except on very hot summer days, a full wetsuit is probably advisable. The action takes place all along the coast, but the epicentre is the stretch between Biarritz and Hossegor. Unless you're a real pro, lessons are strongly recommended – this is not the easiest of sports to master, and the Atlantic is no kiddy pool. Expect to pay around €50 for a day's tuition.

Horse riding

The stunning scenery of this entire region lends itself to gentle, leisurely exploration, and horseback could just be the perfect way to experience it all.

You can take a mule out with you into the Pyrénées (it carries your backpack, not you), or try a horse ride around the vineyards of Sauternes. In the coastal town of Contis-Plage, several horse-riding schools offer gallops along the empty beaches – surely one of the best ways to see and experience the coastline.

Skiing

There are many excellent skiing and snowboarding centres in the Pyrénées, and the relatively low height of the mountains compared to the Alps means there is a great selection of good centres for beginners and families – although keen skiers who want a few thrills won't be disappointed either. Après-ski is not quite as extensive as in the Alps, which may be a drawcard for some skiers, and what you'll find often tends to be centred around the food and wine culture of the area, which is obviously a real bonus. There are certain resorts, such as **Les Angles** or **Ax-3 Domaines**, which do attract a younger and livelier crowd. For a good overview of these and all the 38 ski stations on offer, check out *www.lespyrenees.net* or *www.pyrenees-online.fr*

Golf

Southwest France is also known for its golf courses, and golf lovers will have no trouble finding well-located and well-equipped facilities. In total, there are around 60 courses in this region, and the weather means fairways are permanently green. There is a long history of golf in this area, and **Pau Golf Club** in Billère (*www.paugolfclub.com*) is the oldest in Europe, created for the British Army back in 1856.

Spectator sports

Rugby is the grand passion of most red-blooded southwest males (and plenty of women too), and if you can go to see a game while you are here, it is a highly rewarding experience. Locals are fiercely proud of their teams, but the atmosphere is always friendly and welcoming – if highly charged, particularly if two local teams are playing against each other. Football comes a very close second in terms of loyalty in this part of France (this is the country, after all, that won the World Cup in 1998, the same year that they hosted the tournament), and all the major towns and cities have their own teams.

For tickets to either sport, contact the clubs directly (*see 'Directory', p184*), or go to the local tourist offices, as these often have a ticketing window and will have details of match days and times.

Besides these two, the other big spectator sport in the region is horse jumping, which has particularly lively centres in Bordeaux and the Bassin d'Arcachon. A good website detailing upcoming events is *www.jumping-bordeaux.com*

Cycle along the banks of the Garonne

Children

Besides the obvious attractions that 250km (155 miles) of beach can offer to children, you'll find more than enough to keep little ones occupied around southwest France, from the grottoes and caves in the Dordogne to medieval castles in the Lot and colourful festivals in the Pays Basque. In general, as across much of France, children are warmly welcomed and accommodated for in restaurants and hotels.

Even Michelin-style restaurants often have a gourmet tasting menu for younger visitors, and most cafés are happy to bring blank paper and pens over to the table to keep them entertained during mealtimes. You'll also find that children tend to stay up later in the evenings in this part of the world, often eating with adults, particularly over the summer months.

Exploring Biarritz's rockpools

When it comes to specific attractions, older children will enjoy trying out surfing and sailing along the coast, and almost all of the regional parks have activities on offer from tree-top adventure circuits, like **Jungle Park** in Les Landes (*see 'Directory', p189*), to mountain biking and white-water rafting. In the cities, the **Cité de l'Espace** in Toulouse is a must (*see p90*), while Bordeaux has several excellent museums, alongside cycle and skate parks along the riverbanks, and several large watersports centres both at Bordeaux-Lac (*see p174*) and the **Stade Nautique de Pessac** (*www.stadenautique-de-pessac.fr, see 'Directory', p174*). For something completely different, visit the **Parc de l'Art Préhistorique** (Prehistoric Park) in Tarascon-sur-Ariège (*Tel: 05 61 05 10 10. www.sesta.fr*), where you can learn about the lifestyle of prehistoric man, and any adventurous children can try their hand at making weapons out of silex flint, lighting a fire, throwing a spear or even cave painting!

Cité de l'Espace, Toulouse

For little ones, there are numerous zoos and theme parks. The **Zoo de Bordeaux** in Pessac (*3 chemin du Transvaal, 33600 Pessac. Tel: 05 57 89 28 10. www.zoo-bordeaux-pessac.com. Open: Apr–Sept daily 9.30am–6pm. Admission charge*) is particularly good, with extensive conservation programmes and large-sized enclosures for the animals. In the Pyrénées, **Walibi Aquitaine** is a more traditional theme park, with roller coasters and water rides (*Tel: 05 53 96 58 47. www.walibi-aquitaine.fr. Admission charge*). Other animal parks include **La Pinède des Singes**, where macaque monkeys run free among the pine trees of the Pyrénées-Atlantiques (*RN10, 40530 Labenne. Tel: 05 59 45 43 66. www.pinede-des-singes.com. Open: Apr–Sept Mon, Tue, Thur & Fri 2–6pm, Wed, Sat & Sun 11am–6pm. Admission charge*), and the beautiful **Le Moulin de Poyaller** in the Landes (*Tel: 05 58 97 95 72. www.moulin-poyaller.com. Admission charge*), a medieval mill and nature park where you will see white stags and fallow deer alongside wallabies and alpacas. And the **Miroir d'Eau** in central Bordeaux (*see p36*) guarantees hours of fun for adults and children alike.

Any time you are doing outside activities, do remember that the sun can get extremely hot in this part of France, and protective clothing and hats should be used at all times, even in cities. If you're travelling with babies, pharmacies can be convenient places to get nappies and baby food (always check the label of the food to ensure there is nothing your child is allergic to). When breastfeeding young babies, use your discretion and be sensitive, as it is fairly unusual to see French mothers breastfeeding in public.

Essentials

Arriving and departing
By air
Well served by regional, national
and international flights (*see below*),
the main airports in southwest France
are Toulouse-Blagnac, Bordeaux-
Mérignac, Bergerac, Pau, Agen,
Brive and Périgueux. Flight times
from London vary depending on
destination, but should all be under
two hours.

You may be interested in lessening
the environmental impact of your
flight through **Climate Care**
(*www.climatecare.org*), which offsets
your CO_2 by funding environmental
projects around the world.
Aer Lingus *Tel: 01 70 20 00 72.*
www.aerlingus.ie
Air France *Tel: 08 20 82 08 20.*
www.airfrance.fr
BMI *Tel: 01 41 91 87 04.*
www.flybmi.com
British Airways *Tel: 08 25 82 54 00.*
www.britishairways.com
easyJet *Tel: 08 25 08 25 08.*
www.easyjet.com

By sea
For southwest France, the closest port
to receive cross-Channel traffic is Saint-
Malo, five hours' drive from Bordeaux.
Le Havre is six hours away. Another
alternative is to take a ferry to
Santander in Spain and drive
northwards from there.

Brittany Ferries
www.brittanyferries.com
P&O Ferries *www.poferries.com*

By car
From Paris, the A1 motorway heads
down to southwest France as far as
Bordeaux, where the A63 motorway
branches off westwards towards the
Bassin d'Arcachon and then down to
Biarritz and the French Pyrénées.
Continuing south, the A62 motorway
leads to Toulouse, down to Carcassonne
and over to Montpellier. Heading
eastwards into the Dordogne, the A89
takes you to Périgueux and continues
on towards the Massif Central, passing
Libourne and Saint-Émilion. Drive
time from Paris to Bordeaux is five or
six hours, with another two hours to
Toulouse. Traffic information is
available at *www.infotrafic.com*

By coach
Europe's largest coach operator,
Eurolines, serves all of France
(*www.eurolines.com*).

By train
From London Waterloo via Eurostar to
Paris Gare du Nord, and then by TGV
to Bordeaux or Toulouse, takes about
ten hours (trains run regularly
throughout the day). Return fares are
often great value. Good regional trains
cover travel within the southwest.

Within the UK, **Eurostar reservations**
(*Tel: 08705 186 186. www.eurostar.com*).
Within France, **SNCF reservations**
(*Tel: 08 92 35 35 35. www.sncf.com*).

Customs

Residents of UK, Ireland and other EU
countries may bring into France
personal possessions and 'reasonable
amounts' of goods for personal use,
provided they have been purchased in
the EU. You're allowed 4 litres of wine
and 16 litres of beer plus 1 litre of drink
containing over 22 per cent alcohol and
2 litres of 22 per cent or less, plus 200
cigarettes or 50 cigars. For full
regulations, visit *www.douane.gouv.fr*.
For taking animals to France, EU rules
apply: they need a European (EU) Pet
Passport, and from July 2011 must also
have microchip identification. Your
local vet will have details.

Electricity

France runs on 230V and uses a plug
with two round pins. British appliances
need an adaptor, easily obtained at any
electrical or hardware store, or at the
airport. US and other equipment
designed for 110V needs a transformer.

Embassies and consulates

Australian Embassy. *4 rue Jean Rey,
75724 Paris. Tel: 01 40 59 33 00.*
British Consulate. *353 boulevard
Wilson, 33000 Bordeaux.
Tel: 05 57 22 21 10.*
Canadian Consulate. *10 rue Jules de
Rességuier, 31000 Toulouse.*

Essentials

CONVERSION TABLE

FROM	TO	MULTIPLY BY
Inches	Centimetres	2.54
Feet	Metres	0.3048
Yards	Metres	0.9144
Miles	Kilometres	1.6090
Acres	Hectares	0.4047
Gallons	Litres	4.5460
Ounces	Grams	28.35
Pounds	Grams	453.6
Pounds	Kilograms	0.4536
Tons	Tonnes	1.0160

To convert back, for example from
centimetres to inches, divide by the number
in the third column.

MEN'S SUITS

UK	36	38	40	42	44	46	48
Rest of Europe	46	48	50	52	54	56	58
USA	36	38	40	42	44	46	48

DRESS SIZES

UK	8	10	12	14	16	18
France	36	38	40	42	44	46
Italy	38	40	42	44	46	48
Rest of Europe	34	36	38	40	42	44
USA	6	8	10	12	14	16

MEN'S SHIRTS

UK	14	14.5	15	15.5	16	16.5	17
Rest of Europe	36	37	38	39/40	41	42	43
USA	14	14.5	15	15.5	16	16.5	17

MEN'S SHOES

UK	7	7.5	8.5	9.5	10.5	11
Rest of Europe	41	42	43	44	45	46
USA	8	8.5	9.5	10.5	11.5	12

WOMEN'S SHOES

UK	4.5	5	5.5	6	6.5	7
Rest of Europe	38	38	39	39	40	41
USA	6	6.5	7	7.5	8	8.5

Tel: 05 61 52 19 06.
Open: Mon–Fri 9am–noon.
New Zealand Embassy. *7 rue Léonard de Vinci, 75116 Paris.*
Tel: 01 45 01 43 43.
South African Embassy. *59 quai d'Orsay, 75343 Paris.*
Tel: 01 53 59 23 23.
US Consulate. *25 allées Jean Jaurès, 31000 Toulouse. Tel: 05 34 41 36 50.*
Open: Mon–Fri 9am–5pm.

Emergency numbers
Ambulance *15*
Fire *18*

Police *17*
SOS Europe-wide *112*

Health and insurance
Southwest France is by and large a very safe place for holidays. Drinking water is safe, and many public parks have drinking fountains. (If the water isn't safe to drink, it is labelled 'Eau Non Potable'.) At almost all restaurants, you will be given a *pichet d'eau* when you sit down – a jug of tap water that is perfectly safe.

Specific risks include jellyfish along the Atlantic Coast, and adders when

Bordeaux train station

out walking in country parks. No inoculations are necessary for British citizens travelling to France. If you have any queries, ask your doctor before leaving, or read the Department of Health leaflet T5 'Health Advice for Travellers', available at most UK post offices or at *www.dh.gov.uk*. If you are on regular medication, take enough to last your holiday, as very rural areas may struggle to provide what you need.

Medical facilities in France are excellent, and visitors from the UK are covered by EU reciprocal health schemes while in France (obtain a European Health Insurance Card (EHIC) before leaving home). This guarantees emergency treatments only. All travellers should ensure they have adequate travel insurance that covers medical as well as travel and baggage mishaps.

Internet

There is good Internet access at most hotels, train stations and airports in the main population centres – much of it free Wi-Fi. Rural coverage is less regular, although hotels will usually have at least one connection point.

Medical services

There are casualty departments in all the major towns and cities. Emergency treatment, as with all medical treatment in France, has to be paid up front, and then payment reclaimed through insurance.

The major hospitals include:
Centre Hospitalier de Périgueux.
80 avenue Georges Pompidou, 24000 Périgueux. Tel: 05 53 45 25 25.
Hôpital des Enfants. *330 avenue de Grande Bretagne, 31000 Toulouse. Tel: 05 34 55 86 33.*
Hôpital Pellegrin, CHU (Centre Hospitalier Universitaire) de Bordeaux. *Place Amélie Raba-Léon, 33000 Bordeaux. Tel: 05 56 79 56 79.*
Hôpital Rangueil, CHU de Toulouse.
Avenue Jean Poulhès, 31000 Toulouse. Tel: 05 61 32 25 33.
Polyclinique Aguilera. *21 rue de l'Estagnas, 64200 Biarritz. Tel: 05 59 22 47 47.*

Doctors

If you are in need of medical assistance outside of normal working hours, call **SOS Médecins** (*www.sosmedecins-france.fr*), who will come to your house or hotel.

Money

Currency is the euro, in notes of €5, €10, €20, €50, €100 and €500. Coins are in denominations of €1 and €2, and in centimes worth 1c, 2c, 5c, 10c, 20c and 50c. ATMs are found at many banks and at airports and main railway stations. Most international debit and credit cards are accepted at ATMs and in main shops. Traveller's cheques and foreign money can be cashed at most banks and some hotels. Your passport will be required for ID for most banking transactions.

For up-to-date exchange rates, check *www.travelex.com* or *www.oanda.com*

Opening hours

Banks: Mon–Fri 9am–12.30pm & 2–5pm
Pharmacies: Mon–Sat 8.30/9am–noon & 2–7pm
Restaurants: daily noon–2pm & 7–10.30pm (although some close on Mondays)
Shops: Mon–Sat 9.30/10am–12.30pm & 2–7pm

Passports and visas

EU citizens can travel to France without a visa. For USA, Canada, Australia, New Zealand and South Africa, visits of up to three months do not require a visa, but passports must be valid for at least six months after the date of entry.

Pharmacies

For after-hours, Sunday or bank-holiday help, ask for the *Pharmacie de Garde* (Emergency Pharmacy) at your local tourist office or police station. Alternatively, closed pharmacies will put a sign in their window directing you to the nearest open one.

Post

Post offices sell telephone cards and usually have photocopiers or a fax machine available for public use.

Public holidays

1 January Jour de L'An (New Year's Day)
March/April Lundi de Pâques (Easter Monday)
1 May Fête du Travail (Labour Day)
8 May Victoire 1945 (VE Day)
May/June Ascension
Lundi de Pentecôte (Whit Monday)
14 July La Fête Nationale (Bastille Day)
15 August Assomption (Assumption)
1 November Touissant (All Saints' Day)
11 November Armistice 1918 (World War I Armistice)
25 December Noel (Christmas Day)

Safety and crime

Southwest France is a safe place to visit, but as with anywhere, take care whenever you are travelling with money and passports, particularly in Bordeaux and Toulouse late at night and around the railway station areas. Report any loss or theft immediately upon discovering it, if only for insurance purposes. Police tend to be very helpful (and extremely vigilant on traffic infractions, so don't speed or go through amber traffic lights).

Hôtel de Police, 23 boulevard de l'Embouchure, 31066 Toulouse.
Tel: 05 61 12 77 77.
Hôtel de Police, 23 rue François de Sourdis, 33000 Bordeaux.
Tel: 05 57 85 77 77.

Smoking

This is banned inside restaurants and bars in France, but smoking rooms and outside terraces are still fair game.

Suggested reading and media

The *Sud Ouest* regional newspaper is a good source of news, information and entertainment listings. There are also numerous local magazines that concentrate on the wines, such as *Terre des Vins* (available in newsagents across the region). Iconic reads include *The Three Musketeers* (Alexandre Dumas), *War and Wine* (Donald and Petie Kladstrup) and *Blackberry Wine* (Joanne Harris). Food lovers should try *From Here You Can't See Paris* (Michael Sanders), *Cooking and Travelling in Southwest France* (Stephanie Alexander) and *The Cooking of Southwest France* (Paula Wolfert).

Tax

The standard rate of TVA (Taxe sur la Value Ajoutée, similar to the UK's Value Added Tax) in France is 19.6 per cent, although food is taxed at 5.5 per cent. If you have a valid flight ticket for a non-EU destination, you can buy certain goods free of duty and tax in airports, ports and certain department stores. Ask when purchasing.

Telephones

The area code for southwest France is 05, followed by the local eight-digit number. The area code must be used when dialling from anywhere in France. To call from outside France, dial your own international prefix (00 in most countries) then 33 for France, the area code minus the initial '0', and the local number. Mobile phone coverage is good except in the most remote areas. The main service providers are Bouygues Télécom, Orange and SFR. Public phones are common in the major cities, and require a *télécarte*, available at *tabacs* (newsagents) and pharmacies, or a debit/credit card.

Time

France is GMT +1 hour.

Toilets

Most city centres have public toilets, as do railway stations, airports and most parks, usually pod-style, where a door will automatically open and close upon pressing a button (or putting in a coin). Alternatively, ask at a friendly café if you can use the facilities.

Travellers with disabilities

All major airports and train stations have good access, as do the Bordeaux trams and Toulouse metro. Buses tend to be ill-equipped, and many hotels are not wheelchair-friendly. Useful organisations include:

Association des Paralysés en France. *www.apf.asso.fr*
RADAR. *12 City Forum, 250 City Road, London EC1V 8AF.*
Tel: 020 7250 3222.
www.radar.org.uk
SATH. *347 Fifth Avenue, Suite 610, NY 10016.*

Language

As with any visit to a non-English-speaking country, your experience of the country and people will be greatly enhanced if you have a few basic ideas about the language, and learn in advance a few key phrases that will help you during your stay. As France is a major European country, you are unlikely to run into any major linguistic problems, but it doesn't hurt to be prepared. In the major cities in southwest France, English is fairly widely spoken – certainly in the more touristy areas, where the locals are well used to visitors – but this is less true when you head out into the sparsely populated areas, particularly in the far reaches of the Lot, or up in the mountains of the Pyrénées. The French are very proud of their country and their language, and an effort to speak some French is always appreciated, even if you don't get it right, and even if it does not go far beyond 'please' and 'thank you'.

Worldwide, France is considered the fifth most spoken language in the world, with around 265 million speakers worldwide. It essentially follows the same grammatical rules as English – sentences are usually formed with a subject, a verb and an object – and the basics can be attempted fairly easily. Unlike in English, French-speakers generally use a lot of liaison, where words slide into each other without distinct gaps between them. One way to get a feel for this and for the language in general is to listen to French radio or watch some French television or film, both before you leave and while you are there. Reading through French newspapers is also helpful. Even if you understand only a few words, you'll gain at least a basic understanding of what is happening in the country and what is important to the locals – you can always use some stories you have seen to start up a conversation. And when in doubt, compliment the area that you are in: this is always a good ice-breaker, in any language!

Look the part, too?

A few key phrases, particularly useful for travelling, include the following:

Do you speak English? Parlez-vous anglais? (parlay-voo ahnglay)

I'm sorry, I don't speak French. Je suis désolé, je ne parle pas le français. (zhuh swee dezolay, zhuh ne paarl pa le fransay)

Where is the bus station? Où ce trouve la gare routière? (oo se troov la gaar rootiyair)

Where is the train station? Où ce trouve la gare? (oo se troov la gaar)

Where is the airport? Où ce trouve l'aéroport? (oo se troov l'air-o-por)

The train leaves from platform two. Le train part de quai deux. (le tra paar de kay der)

Where can I get a taxi? Où puis-je trouver un taxi? (oo pooey-zhuh truuvay un taxi?)

Have a good journey! Bon voyage! (bon vwayaazh)

Can I have a table for two please? Une table pour deux, s'il vous plaît. (oon tabl pour der seel voo play)

I'm a vegetarian. Je suis végétarien/ne. (zhuh swee vegetarian/enne)

I have a reservation. J'ai réservé une table. (zhay reservay oon tabl)

Enjoy your meal! Bon appétit! (bon upetee)

I'd like to make a reservation. Je voudrais réserver une table. (zhuh voodray reservay oon tabl)

The bill please. L'addition, s'il vous plaît. (ladeeseeon seel voo play)

Can I pay by card? Puis-je payer avec une carte de crédit? (pooey zhuh payay avec oon cart duh craydee)

That was delicious. C'était délicieux. (saytay daylee seeyur)

Directory

Accommodation price guide

Prices in this guide are based on the cost per person for two people sharing the least expensive double room with en-suite bathroom, where appropriate. Costs may vary significantly with the seasons, peaking in summer holidays.

£	less than €50
££	€51–75
£££	€76–95
££££	over €95

Eating out price guide

Prices are per person for an evening meal without drinks. Many restaurants serve cheaper set menus at lunchtime.

£	less than €30
££	€31–45
£££	€46–75
££££	over €75

BORDEAUX AND VINEYARDS

Bordeaux

ACCOMMODATION

Auberge de la Jeunesse (Youth Hostel) £
Clean and centrally located youth hostel with Internet access and showers in nearly all rooms. There's also satellite TV, and the hostel is next to several good nightspots.
22 rue Barbey. Tel: 05 56 33 00 70. www.auberge-jeunesse-bordeaux.com

Camping Bordeaux Lac £
A new campsite (opened in 2009) that is located in the Bordeaux-Lac area, around 20 minutes from the city centre but with good transport links. It offers good-sized pitches with electricity, water and waste disposal. Open all year and equipped with heating for winter. There are also cabins available to rent.
Boulevard du Parc des Expositions, 33520 Bruges-Bordeaux. Tel: 05 57 87 70 60. www. camping-bordeaux.com. Tram: Parc des Expositions. Exit 5 off the Bordeaux rocade (ring road).

L'Avant-Scène £££
A new, contemporary-style, relaxed hotel opened (July 2009) in the Chartrons district of the city centre. The same owners have two restaurants, one in place Stalingrad in the Bastide sector of Bordeaux, and the other by the beach in Cap Ferret, but the hotel itself just has a breakfast room. Free Wi-Fi.
36 rue Borie. Tel: 05 57 29 25 39. www.lavantscene.fr

The Regent ££££
Great location opposite the Grand Théâtre with 150 rooms and suites, including the largest one in the city, all conceived by celebrated designer Jacques Garcia. Guests should have access to a fully equipped, state-of-the-art spa with swimming pool in 2011, although this has been delayed several

times. Two excellent restaurants also.

2–5 place de la Comédie. Tel: 05 57 30 44 04. www. theregentbordeaux.com

EATING OUT

Le Bistro Régent £

Not connected to the hotel of the same name, there are three lively bistros in this newly opened chain. Your choice is limited to either grilled beef, duck or salmon accompanied by unlimited chips and green salad. Simple, attractively decorated and well priced, these new bistros have become instantly popular, so get there early or book ahead.

Cours Georges Clemenceau / Rue Saint-Rémi / Place de la République. Tel: 05 56 44 90 00. Open: daily noon–2.30pm & 7.30–10.30pm.

L'Huître à Flots £

If you don't have time to drive out to the Bassin d'Arcachon, head over to this wilfully understated restaurant – if you can find it, that is. It's hidden down a forgotten corner of the Bassin à Flot, near to the submarine pens. It's basically an oyster shack, but with a wider menu that includes fish and pasta dishes. And it's great.

Bassin à Flot No 2. Tel: 05 56 39 64 08. Open: Tue–Sat noon–2pm & 7.30–10pm.

Le Brasserie Bordelais ££

Lively restaurant with leanings towards regional food (so plenty of duck and steak). The wine list is excellent, perhaps because one of the owners is a wine consultant.

50 rue Saint-Remi. Tel: 05 57 87 11 91. www. brasseriebordelaise.fr. Open: daily noon–2.30pm & 7.30–10.30pm.

ENTERTAINMENT

CGR Bordeaux

The new CGR cinema in Bordeaux is one of the first digital 3D cinemas in France, housed in a beautifully restored building in the Triangle d'Or.

Rond Point de L'Intendance. Tel: 08 92 68 85 88. www.cgrcinemas.fr

Grand Théâtre

A beautiful theatre building that hosts regular events throughout the year. It's always worth going to the box office to check what is on, and don't forget to ask about their lunchtime recitals, and special events for younger children.

Place de la Comédie. Tel: 05 56 00 85 20. www.opera-bordeaux.com

Rock School Barbey

One of the best places to watch live music in the city, this concert hall, music school and sometimes nightclub is a lively and ever-changing venue. It is also located just down the road from the youth hostel.

18 cours Barbey. Tel: 05 56 33 66 00. www.rockschool-barbey.com

UGC Ciné Cité Bordeaux

For English-language films, this is still the best place to see films in their 'Version Originale'.

13/15 rue Georges Bonnac. www.ugc.fr

Utopia

A great cinema for arts and festival films.
5 place Camille Jullian.
Tel: 05 56 52 00 15.
www.cinemas-utopia.org

SPORT AND LEISURE

Centre de Voile Bordeaux-Lac

Windsurfing and sailing centre at a lake just outside the city centre of Bordeaux. There is also a beach-volley court, a hiking trail and a beach just alongside.
Boulevard Parc des Expositions, 33520 Bruges. Tel: 05 57 10 60 35. Tram: Parc des Expositions.

Piscine Judaïque

This beautiful Art Deco public pool dates from the 1930s but was renovated in 2008 (with further renovations to the largest pool continuing until early 2011). There are several pools, one with a waterslide, and another that is outdoors for hot summer days. Remember that swimming caps must be worn in all public pools in France, and men should wear speedos not swimming trunks.
166 rue Judaïque. Tel: 05 56 51 48 31.
www.bordeaux.fr. Open: hours vary, so call ahead or check website for details. Bus: 1, 16.

Le Stade Nautique de Pessac

Outdoor and indoor swimming pools are at this extensive waterpark a few kilometres from Bordeaux centre.
Avenue des Acieries, 33600 Pessac. Tel: 05 56 07 12 78. www.stadenautique-de-pessac.fr. Open: daily 10am–7.45pm, but hours vary, so check website for details. Tram: Line B to Pessac Centre, then Bus 47.

BORDEAUX VINEYARDS

Arsac

EATING OUT

Le Wy £££

This restaurant is located in La Winery, the innovative wine centre on the D1 road up to Moulis and Listrac. There is a huge wine list with tipples from all over France, and some good choices by the glass. There is also a tapas bar for lighter (and cheaper) meals.
Rond Point des Vendangeurs, 33460 Arsac. Tel: 05 56 39 04 91. www.la-winery.com. Open: daily noon–2pm & 7.30–10pm.

Blaye

ACCOMMODATION

Villa-Saint-Simon £

The South-African owner makes this a very welcoming place to stay, within a few minutes' walk of the citadel and port. All rooms are decorated very traditionally, and you'll find various antiques tucked into hidden corners.
8 cours du Général de Gaulle, 33390 Blaye. Tel: 05 57 42 99 66. www.bordeauxwinevilla.com

Camblanes-et-Meynac

EATING OUT

La Maison du Fleuve £££

Around 20 minutes from central Bordeaux, on the attractive D10 road, this smart restaurant serves imaginative food and

wine, and has a terrace overlooking the Garonne river. They make full use of the river by having their own jetty: a boat will take you there and back from Bordeaux city centre every Thursday evening, from May to September (book through the restaurant).
20 chemin Seguin, Port Neuf, 33360 Camblanes-et-Meynac. Tel: 05 56 20 06 40. www.maison-du-fleuve.com. Open: Tue–Sun noon–2pm & 7.30–10pm.

Listrac-Médoc
ACCOMMODATION
Les Cinq Sens, Château Mayne-Lalande ££–£££
A new *chambre d'hôtes* that has opened recently at Château Mayne-Lalande, housed in a separate building opposite the main winery. This offers a great opportunity to stay in a winery, where you can do tastings and tours, and get to know the area with real experts. There is also a small spa.
Route du Mayne, 33480 Listrac-Médoc. Tel: 05 56 58 27 63. www.chateau-mayne-lalande.com

Le Pian-Médoc
ACCOMMODATION
Natura Cabana, Château Malleret ££
For something totally different, you can choose to stay in one of five tree-top rooms in the grounds of Château Malleret near Pian-Médoc, just at the start of the Route des Châteaux. The tree houses are around 6m (20ft) off the ground, and you have to bring your own bedding, but they are located in a large park, with beautiful views, and are heated when the weather is cold.
75 rue La Fontaine, 33290 Le Pian-Médoc. Tel: 05 56 46 29 48. www.naturacabana.fr

Saint-Émilion
ACCOMMODATION
Le Relais Franc Mayne £££
Château Franc Mayne is a Saint-Émilion Grand Cru Classé wine estate that dates from the 16th century. Nine differently themed rooms range from 'Asian mood' to 'Pop art'. There is a natural swimming pool in the attractive gardens. A *table d'hôte* evening meal also offers good-quality food, but book ahead.
14 La Gomerie, 33330 Saint-Émilion. Tel: 05 57 24 62 61. www. relaisfrancmayne.com

Saint-Germain-du-Puch
EATING OUT
L'Atmosphère ££
In a pretty village right in the heart of Entre-Deux-Mers, wooden tables, a large terrace, jazz music and friendly staff all mean this place more than lives up to the name. It offers excellent-quality food, with a mix of pizza and pasta plus inventive takes on local dishes.
99 Le Bourg, 33750 Saint-Germain-du-Puch. Tel: 05 57 24 52 34. Open: daily noon–2pm & 8–10pm.

THE ATLANTIC COAST
Biarritz
ACCOMMODATION
Hôtel Palacito ££–£££
A chic and crisply

designed hotel, with plenty of quirky touches, it's well located close to the beach and the shops. A good bar on the ground floor serves cocktails in the evening.
1 rue Gambetta. Tel: 05 59 24 04 89. www.palacito.com

EATING OUT
Blue Cargo £
Join the young crowd by heading over to this near-perfect beachside hangout, which has a good restaurant, a terrace that is literally on the beach, and a bar and club that is open until 2am throughout the summer.
Avenue d'Ilbarritz, Bidart. Tel: 05 59 23 54 87. www.bluecargo.fr. Open: restaurant Jul–Aug daily 11.30am–4.30pm & 7.30–9.30pm; rest of the year 11.30am–4.30pm; nightclub open summer months only.

Chez Albert ££
Overlooking the fishing port, life will seem pretty sweet on a warm summer's evening at this excellent fish restaurant.
Allée Port des Pêcheurs. Tel: 05 59 24 43 84.

www.chezalbert.fr. Open: Thur–Tue (Jul–Aug daily) 12.15–2pm & 7.30–10pm.

SPORT AND LEISURE
Biarritz Paradise Surf School
You are going to come across dozens of surf shops and surf training centres all along the main seafront in Biarritz, as well as in every small village within spitting distance. This is one of the best, offering plenty of equipment and training courses. Everything from casual lessons to intensive week-long courses, and they can organise accommodation also.
8 passage Latuillke. Tel: 06 14 76 01 18. www.biarritzparadisesurf school.com

Cap Ferret
ACCOMMODATION
Hôtel des Dunes ££
Renovated in 2006, this offers a slightly less expensive way to stay in Cap Ferret, and is closer to the ocean side of the peninsula. You still get the same shabby-chic beachfront feel, with

plenty of exposed natural wood and a good terrace.
119 avenue de Bordeaux, 33970 Lège-Cap-Ferret. Tel: 05 56 60 61 81. www.hoteldesdunes.com

Maison du Bassin ££££
New England rustic chic is the order of the day at this charming hotel. There's an excellent restaurant and bar (they make their own rums, so be sure to order a Mojito) and the rooms are all casually expensive. Located very close to the oyster village.
5 rue des Pionniers, 33970 Lège-Cap-Ferret. Tel: 05 56 60 60 63. www. lamaisondubassin.com

EATING OUT
Bouchon du Ferret ££
A new restaurant that has opened recently in the oyster village at the tip of Cap Ferret, owned by the same team who owns Brasserie Bordelais in Bordeaux city.
Chez Boulon, 2 rue des Palmiers, Quartier Ostreicole, Lège-Cap-Ferret. Tel: 05 56 60 67 51. Open: daily noon–3pm & 7.30–10.30pm.

Chez Hortense ££

The classic Cap Ferret experience can be had at this beachside restaurant on the edge of the most expensive real estate in the area (known as the '44 Hectares'). Somehow it manages to retain a feeling of easy-going summertime welcome. Order the *moules-frites,* as they are the speciality of the house.

Avenue du Sémaphore, 33950 Lège-Cap-Ferret. Tel: 05 56 60 62 56. Open: Apr–Oct daily noon–2pm & 7–11pm.

ENTERTAINMENT

Sail Fish

A lively restaurant that has music and a bar until late, providing one of the few exciting nightspots in Cap Ferret.

Rue des Bernaches, 33950 Lège-Cap-Ferret. Tel: 05 56 60 44 84.

SPORT AND LEISURE

Bateliers Arcachon

For boat trips around the Bassin d'Arcachon, head to the pier either in Arcachon or Cap Ferret village, where boats run daily to the Île aux Oiseaux, the Banc d'Arguin or around the oyster beds. Some trips offer oysters on board, along with local wine.

76 boulevard de la Plage, 33120 Arcachon. Tel: 05 57 72 28 28. www. bateliers-arcachon.com

Flyway

To try your hand at kite-surfing (which can be physically demanding and fairly hair-raising at times), try a class with this company. Run by expert Eric Platel, it offers good training along the beaches of the Arcachon bay (in the village of Claouey), and also in Andernos.

Tel: 06 61 57 79 79. www.flyway.fr

Capbreton-Hossegor

ACCOMMODATION

Camping La Pointe £

There's easy access to surfing beaches at this campsite, which also has a pool and permanent cabins to rent if you don't want to pitch a tent. The campsite is in a pine forest, but just 800m (875 yards) from the beach.

40130 Capbreton-Hossegor. Tel: 05 58 72 14 98. www.camping-lapointe.com

Hôtel L'Ocean ££

Just 100m (110 yards) from the sea and a white-sand beach, with lovely views from the bedrooms, this is an inexpensive choice of hotel with a reasonable restaurant. There are 24 rooms, and although a little impersonal, it has good access to all the amenities of the area.

85 avenue Georges Pompidou, 40130 Capbreton-Hossegor. Tel: 05 58 72 10 22.

SPORT AND LEISURE

Natural Surf Lodge

A surf camp located in the middle of a nature reserve but close to Capbreton and Hossegor, where everything has been created to ensure minimum impact on the surrounding environment (so you'll find geothermal heating and locally sourced building materials). Owners Claire and Stephane put you up for the week, and teach you to surf.

40510 Seignosse.
Tel: 06 74 16 02 28.
Email: claire@
naturalsurflodge.com.
www.
naturalsurflodge.com

Contis-Plage
ACCOMMODATION
Hotel de la Plage ££
Laid-back, with a lovely
holiday feel and plenty of
chic touches, this
excellent hotel is minutes
from the beach, and has
a good bistro attached
(ask for a table on the
terrace, where you have a
view of the ocean). The
whole place is built out
of wood, in the style
of a traditional
Landais house.
Avenue de l'Ocean.
Tel: 05 58 42 70 15.
www.hotelplagecontis.com

Guéthary
ACCOMMODATION
Hôtel Arguibel £££
Heading down the
Atlantic Coast towards
Saint-Jean-de-Luz, this
lovely boutique hotel in a
charming fishing village
combines highly
designed rooms (you
could easily be in Paris or
Madrid) with a peaceful

setting and several
excellent restaurants
nearby.
Chemin de Laharraga.
Tel: 05 59 41 90 46.
www.arguibel.fr

EATING OUT
Briketenia £££
It might be harder to get
a table since this place
was awarded its first
Michelin star in 2010,
but it's worth trying.
Fantastic regional cuisine
with a deft touch.
Rue de L'Empereur.
Tel: 05 59 26 51 34.
www.briketenia.com.
Open: Wed–Mon
12.30–2pm & 8–9.30pm.

Gujan-Mestras
EATING OUT
Cabanne 118 £
A low-key and
inexpensive oyster hut –
this is what the Bassin
d'Arcachon is all about.
118 port de la Barbotière,
Digue Est.
Tel: 06 84 98 06 84.

ENTERTAINMENT
La Coccinelle
Small, easy to get around
and very low-key, this
animal park provides a
great day out for younger

children. You pay one
price for entry, and the
petting farm (where
children can feed
animals, and give milk
bottles to piglets and
calves depending on the
time of year) and variety
of games and rides are all
included.
33460 Gujan-Mestras.
Tel: 05 56 66 30 41.
www.la-coccinelle.fr.
Open: daily 9am–6pm.
Admission charge.

Hourtin-Plage
ACCOMMODATION
**Camping Côte
d'Argent £**
A large and well-
equipped campsite by the
Hourtin lake, so with
good access to the Médoc
vineyards, but also just
300m (330 yards) from
the Atlantic Coast
beaches.
33990 Hourtin-Plage.
Tel: 05 56 09 10 25.
www.camping-cote-
dargent.com

Pyla-sur-Mer
ACCOMMODATION
**Hôtel de la Corniche
££££**
Head up the glamour
scale at this excellent new

hotel, opened by über-designer Philippe Starck in 2010 and easily one of the best places to stay along the entire Atlantic Coast. It's not cheap, but you get to swim in an infinity pool that overlooks the Bassin d'Arcachon as it heads out to the Atlantic Ocean, and you are right next to the Dune de Pyla, not far from Arcachon. There's also a good restaurant, favoured by Bordeaux's beautiful people.
46 boulevard Louis Gaume.
Tel: 05 56 22 72 11.
www.hoteldelacorniche.fr

Saint-Jean-de-Luz
ACCOMMODATION
Hôtel Villa Bel Air ££
Not the most luxurious of hotels, but excellently located overlooking the beautiful sweep of the bay, right next to all the main beaches and shopping streets. Of the 21 bedrooms, most look out over the sea, but request a sea view in advance to make sure.
60 promenade Jacques Thibaud. Tel: 05 59 26 04 86. www.hotel-bel-air.fr

EATING OUT
La Txalupa £££
The fish soup is the thing to try at this pretty restaurant with a terrace overlooking the port. Most of the menu is centred round seafood, and the majority of it has been freshly caught that morning (the name is Basque for 'small boat').
Place Louis XIV.
Tel: 05 59 51 85 52.

THE FRENCH PYRÉNÉES
Ainhoa
ACCOMMODATION
Hotel Agri-Eder ££
Traditional Basque house in a lovely green spot, close to the centre of this beautiful village. Chalet-style rooms, and excellent food (let them know ahead of time that you would like to eat).
Route de la Chapelle.
Tel: 05 59 93 72 00.
Open: Apr–Nov.

Argelès-Gazost
SPORT AND LEISURE
Parc Animalier des Pyrénées
An unusual stop is found at this park, where over 100 species of wild animal from the area of the Pyrénées are gathered, from bears to marmots to eagles. This is far more than just a wildlife park: it's a genuine centre for conservation, and a fascinating place in which to learn about the ecosystem of the mountains.
60 bis avenue des Pyrénées. Tel: 05 62 97 91 07. www.parc-animalier-pyrenees.com. Open: Apr–Sept daily 9.30am–6pm; Oct 1.30–6pm. Admission charge. Train: to Lourdes, then a navette bus.

Bayonne
ACCOMMODATION
Auberge de Jeunesse, Anglet £
This is 5km (3 miles) away from Bayonne, but makes a good, inexpensive base for exploring the Pyrénées, and has the advantage of also being near to the coast and 5km (3 miles) from Biarritz airport. A popular hangout with surfers, who can also organise surfing lessons for the uninitiated.

19 route des Vignes, 64600 Anglet.
Tel: 05 59 58 70 07.
Email: anglet@fuaj.org

EATING OUT

Mona Lisa ££

This Baroque-style restaurant overlooks the River Nive. Inside, there are comfy armchairs and a few dramatic touches, and a menu of very good Italian food.
54–56 quai des Corsaires.
Tel: 05 56 59 48 31.

Talaia ££

Excellent spot, right on the banks of the Adour river, this *peniche* boat has a lovely bar and restaurant that offers good food – mainly river fish and seafood, as well as a cocktail bar in the evenings.
Quai Pedros.
Tel: 05 59 44 08 84.

Cambo-les-Bains

EATING OUT

Restaurant Le Bellevue ££

Part of a lovely hotel, this restaurant specialises in spa-style cuisine, so expect imaginative, lighter-style food using local ingredients. Chef Gilles Fontanille changes the menu weekly, choosing the best of the local market produce. The restaurant looks out over the Nive valley.
Allée Rostand.
www.hotel-bellevue64.fr.
Open: daily noon–2pm & 7.30–9pm.

Cauterets

ACCOMMODATION

Le Pas de l'Ours £–££

This old-fashioned, basic but very friendly hotel and *gîte* in the centre of Cauterets makes an excellent base for hiking, skiing or generally exploring the region. They offer special stays combining spas with visits to local food producers and artisans. A wood-panelled, Alpine-lodge-style restaurant serves regional cuisine.
21 rue de la Raillière.
Tel: 05 62 92 58 07.
www.lepasdelours.com

Hôtel du Pont d'Espagne ££

You will have to look long and hard to find a better-located hotel and restaurant than this, right by the Pont d'Espagne bridge and beauty spot. Pack your hiking boots and binoculars.
Quartier Pont d'Espagne.
Tel: 05 62 92 54 10.
www.hotel-du-pont-despagne.fr

SPORT AND LEISURE

Lechêne des Montagnes

A safe way to experience the mountains year-round is by going with an experienced guide. Jean-Louis Lechêne has lived in the area for over 20 years, and was the first to open an independent ski school in the Pyrénées. Today he also takes out hiking groups in summer, and can regale you with plenty of grisly tales.
8 rue de Verdun.
Tel: 05 62 92 59 83. www. lechenedesmontagnes.com

Ciboure

ACCOMMODATION

La Croix Basque £

On the first slopes of the Pyrénées as they rise out of Saint-Jean-de-Luz, this is a fantastic place to stay, standing out among the many charming spots in the French Pyrénées. A traditional Basque stone house, with wooden shutters and plenty of shaded balconies for respite on hot days, it also has extensive gardens surrounding the house, and stunning views from pretty much all sides. Well-decorated bedrooms, too.

19 avenue des Pyrénées. Tel: 05 59 47 18 37. Email: lacroixbasque@free.fr. www.lacroixbasque.com

Espelette

ACCOMMODATION

Hôtel Euzkadi ££

A Basque-style house with white walls and red wooden shutters, this hotel is warm and welcoming, and makes for a brilliant stay. Five generations of the same family have run this place, and you will quickly understand why they didn't want to leave. There is a very good restaurant, a nice pool and bags of charm.

285 route Karrika Nagusia. Tel: 05 59 93 91 88. www.hotel-restaurant-euzkadi.com

Louhossoa

SPORT AND LEISURE

Loisirs.64

Canoeing, kayaking, swimming and rafting are on offer at this excellent spot around 15 minutes inland from the coast. If you would prefer to stay on dry land, they can also organise mountain biking and hiking.

64250 Louhossoa. Tel: 05 59 93 35 65. www.loisirs64.com. Admission charge.

Lourdes

ACCOMMODATION

Anousta £

Set around 3km (1¾ miles) from the centre of Lourdes, this charming *chambre d'hôtes* is part of a working farm, with sheep, chickens and geese. It's perfect for people who want to avoid the Lourdes crowds, particularly at times of religious festivals.

28 route de Bartres, 65100 Loubajac. Tel: 05 62 94 44 17. Email: Nadine.vives@wanadoo.fr. www.anousta.com. Open: Feb–Nov.

Les Hauts Pâturages £

Enjoy a stunning location at this *chambre d'hôtes* that also offers *gîte*-style accommodation. Set at an elevation of 700m (2,295ft) between Lourdes (15 minutes away) and the Pic du Midi, the traditional low-stone house is surrounded by total tranquillity. Expect big hearty breakfasts here, perfect for a day out hiking in the mountains.

Ossun ez Angles, 65100 Hautes-Pyrénées. Tel: 05 62 92 57 73. Email: contactfrance@gite-hp.com. www.gite-hp.fr

Pau

ACCOMMODATION

Hôtel Bristol ££

A suitably English name for this most English of French cities. The hotel is well located near to the Château de Henri IV and the Palais des Congrès. Recently renovated and redecorated, it has a smart and elegant dining room for breakfast, and a terrace for summer mornings.

3 rue Gambetta. Tel: 05 59 27 72 98. www.hotelbristol-pau.com

EATING OUT

La Table d'Hôte ££

Enjoy good service and fresh seasonal food at this classic restaurant. It's nicely located in the Old Town of Pau, and the owners, Martine et Fabric Juzanx, have made this one of the most reliable places to eat around here, with plenty of imaginative takes on regional cuisine, from Juraçon sorbets to *foie-gras* in Armagnac.

1 rue du Hédas. Tel: 05 59 27 56 06. Open: daily noon–2pm & 7.30–10pm.

SPORT AND LEISURE

Pau Golf Club 1856

The oldest golf club in continental Europe, opened by two Scottish officers in 1856 who were stationed in Pau after the Napoleonic Wars. There is a very attractive Victorian-style clubhouse and restaurant (for members or guests), and the whole place has a wonderfully old-school atmosphere. Golfing enthusiasts who are not members are permitted access, as are beginners who undertake the initiation classes.

Rue du Golf, 64140 Billère. Tel: 05 59 13 18 56. Email: contact@paugolfclub.com. www.paugolfclub.com

Saint-Jean-Pied-de-Port

ACCOMMODATION

Hôtel des Remparts £

Stay in a traditional 16th-century Basque-style house, close to the centre of this impossibly picturesque town. There is a restaurant also at the hotel, serving traditional regional cuisine, much of it made with produce from local farmers.

64220 Saint-Jean-Pied-de-Port. Tel: 05 59 37 13 79. Email: remparts. hotel@wanadoo.fr

Camping Narbaitz £–££

There are two campsites near to Saint-Jean-Pied-de-Port, and both are good options for budget stays. This one has a heated pool and is surrounded by vineyards and trout streams, making it an idyllic place to spend some time.

Route de Bayonne, Ascarat. Tel: 05 59 37 21 42. www.campings-paysbasque.com

EATING OUT

Iratze Ostatua ££

Heaven for gourmets, the menu here runs the full gamut of Basque specialities, from local cheeses and *charcuterie* to *gâteau Basque* and the delicious local cider. The menu changes daily according to seasonal produce. And on top of all this, it is very reasonably priced.

11 rue de la Citadelle. Tel: 05 59 49 17 09. http://iratze.zeblog.com

TOULOUSE AND THE TARN

Toulouse

ACCOMMODATION

Hôtel du Taur ££

Well placed high above the Place du Capitole, all bedrooms overlook a quiet central courtyard. This is pretty basic stuff, but clean and tidy.

2 rue du Taur. Tel: 05 61 21 17 54. www.hotel-du-taur.com. Metro: Capitole.

Hotel des Beaux-Arts £££

A great little hotel, perfectly located by Pont Neuf, with many rooms offering views of the river. The rooms are small, but they are very well decorated and the staff are friendly. An excellent bistro is attached to the hotel (well frequented by the wider Toulouse population, so it makes sense to book through the front desk).
1 place du Pont Neuf. Tel: 05 34 45 42 42. www.hoteldesbeauxarts. com. Metro: Esquirol.

EATING OUT
La Réserve £
An airy, welcoming and modern space, which gets buzzy almost every evening. A good range of pizzas and pastas in the heart of the Old Town.
8 rue Jean Suau. Tel: 05 61 21 84 00. www.lareserve-resto.com. Open: daily noon–2.30pm & 7–10.30pm. Bus: 53, 54, 56. Metro: Esquirol, then a 10-minute walk.
Michel Sarran £££
With an increasingly

lauded chef, this restaurant is slightly out of the city centre, but well worth the detour. Small and intimate, it has an excellent wine list that concentrates almost entirely on southwest names. Book ahead.
21 boulevard Armand Duportal. Tel: 05 61 12 32 32. www.michel-sarran.com. Open: Mon–Fri noon–1.45pm & 8–9.45pm.

ENTERTAINMENT
Le Bikini
If you are looking for live music in Toulouse, this should be your first stop. Based just out of the centre in the student-friendly Saint-Agne district. Concerts throughout the week – and often international names.
Rue Théodore Monod, Parc Technologique du Canal, 31520 Ramonville-Saint-Agne. Tel: 05 62 24 09 50. www.lebikini.com
Théâtre du Capitole
Classical music concerts, choral recitals, opera, ballet and plenty more at this beautiful central concert hall in Toulouse.

Place du Capitole. Tel: 05 61 22 31 31; tickets 05 61 63 13 13. www.theatre-du-capitole.fr. Open: see website for programme.

SPORT AND LEISURE
L'Aéroclub Air France de Toulouse
It's hardly suprising that in this city where so much of the history of aviation happened, there are plenty of clubs where you can get skyward yourself. This is one of the most established.
4 avenue Jean-René Lagasse, 31130 Balma. Tel: 05 61 34 85 11. www.acaf-toulouse.com
Piscine d'Été
The Nakache indoor pool is used year-round, but the real discovery is the Parc des Sports with its Piscine d'Été (Summer Pool), complete with faux-rockeries and 1950s architecture.
Allée Gabriel-Biénès. Tel: 05 61 22 31 35. Open: school holidays daily 9am–7pm; rest of the year Mon–Fri 4–7pm, weekends 10am–12.30pm & 3–7pm. Bus: 12, 92.

Stade Toulousain

Rugby is the big spectator sport around here, and you'll find the locals fiercely proud of their team, Stade Toulousain (and not without reason, having won the European championship three times in recent years – in 1996, 2003 and 2005). The biggest matches are played at the Stadium Municipal de Toulouse, although the home stadium has been recently renovated and holds almost 20,000 spectators.

Stade Ernest Wallen, 114 rue Troenes. Tel: 08 92 69 31 15 (€0.15 per minute). www.stadetoulousain.fr. Metro: Arenas. By car: exit 24 Empalot from the Périphérique ring road.

Toulouse FC

Le TéFéCé (or Les Violets, as the local football team is affectionately known – they wear a purple and white kit) has had a few successful seasons recently, after a long spell out in the wilderness. The Stadium Municipal has a capacity of over 35,000 and was one of the key stages in the 1998 World Cup – and will be again in Euro 2016.

Stadium Municipal de Toulouse, Île du Ramier, allée Gabriel-Biénès. www.tfc.info. Bus: 92 (right bank), 12, 52 (left bank).

VéloToulouse

This is the newest way to get around Toulouse – simply pick up a bike from one of the many stations around the city centre (there are 242 in total) and pay as you go (with the first half-hour free). You just need a credit card.

Tel: 08 00 11 22 05. www.velo.toulouse.fr. Open: telephone info Mon–Fri 8am–7pm, Sat 8am–6pm, Sun 9am–6pm; bike hire is available 5.30am–2am, with returns possible 24 hours a day.

Albi

ACCOMMODATION

Camping de Caussels £

Just a few kilometres outside of town, this very basic campsite makes a good base for exploring the region, if you don't mind roughing it for a day or two.

Route de Millau, 81000 Albi. Tel: 05 63 60 37 06.

Hôtel George V £

Friendly hotel with good-sized rooms, far nicer than most hotels that are placed so near the bus and train stations.

27–29 avenue Maréchal Joffre. Tel: 05 63 54 24 16. www.hotelgeorgev.com

Villa Bellevue £

For a real homespun experience, try this lovely *chambre d'hôtes*, housed in a red-brick building built at the turn of the 20th century. Five minutes on foot from the Old Town of Albi, its rooms are simple but all individually decorated, and the welcome is friendly and helpful.

21 rue de Bitche. Tel: 06 08 70 29 75. www.villabellevue.fr

Le Vieil Alby ££

Small, good-value rooms at this very central hotel, but what really works here is the restaurant, where you can eat fantastic food – always seasonal.

25 rue Henri de Toulouse-Lautrec.

Tel: 05 63 54 14 69.
www.levieilalby.com

EATING OUT
La Calèche £
It's among the French bistro classics, and you'll find a few good vegetarian platters here too.
6 rue de la Piale. Tel: 05 63 54 15 52. Open: daily noon–2pm & 8–10.30pm.

La Réserve £££
In a very attractive setting, this upmarket restaurant (there are also rooms if you want to stay here) has a gorgeous terrace on the banks of the Tarn river. The extensive wine list makes the most of local producers from Gaillac, and it offers excellent seasonal cuisine. Great for a splurge.
Route des Cordes.
Tel: 05 63 60 80 80.
www.lareservealbi.com.
Open: Mon–Sat noon–2pm & 7.30–9.30pm, Sun noon–2pm.

ENTERTAINMENT
Théâtre Municipal d'Albi
A very attractive theatre that stages regular concerts and ballets. It is part of a vibrant arts programme known as the Scène Nationale d'Albi, which hosts events throughout the year in various locations around the city.
Théâtre, rue Saint-Antoine.
Tel: 05 63 54 00 25.
Scène Nationale, place de l'Amitiés entre les Peuples.
Tel: 05 63 38 55 56.
www.sn-albi.fr

Castres
SPORT AND LEISURE
Elastic Jump
Thrill-seekers get ready, as bungee-jumping has now reached this calm, quiet part of southwest France. Most jumping takes place near Castres, off Le Pont de Bezergue, about 90 minutes from Toulouse city centre.
8 impasse de San Marino, 33140 Pechbonnieu. Tel: 05 61 74 64 00. Email: elasticjump@free.fr.
www.elasticjump.com

Cordes-sur-Ciel
ACCOMMODATION
Hostellerie du Vieux Cordes £££
A well-located and welcoming hotel that is both elegant and spacious. Good-sized bedrooms, each individually decorated, and a good restaurant which serves dishes based around two local specialities: salmon from the local rivers, and the ubiquitous southwest duck. Free Wi-Fi, too. This is part of the Yves Thuriès empire in Cordes, so you will also find a more expensive restaurant of his nearby, and plenty of access to his wonderful chocolates – gourmet heaven!
Haut-de-la-Cité. Tel: 05 63 53 79 20.
www.vieuxcordes.fr

Gaillac
ACCOMMODATION
Camping Gaillac £
Right in the heart of the Gaillac vineyards, this green and very quiet campsite has a few chalets for hire as well as generously sized pitches for tents. There is a pool and a small snack bar, and plenty of opportunities to organise wine tastings, hiking and boat trips in the surrounding area.

9 avenue Guynemer.
Tel: 05 63 57 18 30.
www.camping-gaillac.fr

EATING OUT
La Falaise ££
You can eat outside
beneath huge old trees in
the lovely courtyard at
this restaurant in the
heart of the Gaillac wine
routes.
Routes de Cordes,
Cahuzac sur Vere.
Tel: 05 63 33 96 31. www.
lafalaiserestaurant.com.
Open: Tue 7.30–10.30pm,
Wed–Sun noon–1.30pm
& 7.30–10.30pm.

LA DORDOGNE AND LE LOT

Bergerac
EATING OUT
Restaurant La Cocotte des Halles £
Fresh fish, daily market
produce, all at an
excellent price, this is a
great place for lunch –
and people-watching, as
it is located near the
market. There is a terrace
for outside eating.
14 place du Marché
Couvert. Tel: 05 53 24 10
00. Open: Mon–Sat
11.30am–2pm (daily
Jul–Aug).

Cahors
ACCOMMODATION
La Bergerie ££
Five minutes from
downtown Cahors, this
simple but friendly hotel
has lovely gardens and a
good pool with excellent
views. Chef Joël Gilbert
concentrates on
regional food.
Route de Brive, D820,
46090 Saint-Pierre-
Lafeuillle. Tel: 05 65 36 82
82. www.labergerie-
lot.com

EATING OUT
Le Marché £££
With refined food from
chef Hervé Bourg, this is
a creative restaurant that
makes for a real treat.
Expect dishes such as
tartare of tomatoes or
foie gras with fig, and an
unbelievably tasty range
of desserts. An in-house
deli means you can bring
some of his wonderful
cooking back home
with you.
27 place Chapou.
Tel: 05 65 35 27 27.
www.
restaurantlemarche.com.
Open: Tue–Sat
noon–2pm; for evening
dining, call ahead.

Cieurac
EATING OUT
La Table de Haute-Serre £££
A very good restaurant
housed in an attractive
stone cellar. The owner,
Georges Vigouroux, is a
well-known local wine
producer (he also owns
another upmarket local
hotel-restaurant called
Château de Mercues,
www.chateaudemercues.
com), and this is reflected
in the wine list and in the
emphasis on matching
food and wine. Over the
winter months, expect
truffles to feature very
heavily on the menu.
Château de Haute-Serre.
Tel: 05 65 20 80 20.
www.hauteserre.fr. Open:
daily noon–2pm &
8–10pm.

Issigeac
ACCOMMODATION
Château Gauthié ££
Tree-houses are on offer
here, in a lovely country
house not far from the
medieval village of
Issigeac. You can choose
from two cabins: a
romantic retreat for two,
or a larger wood cabin
for two to five people. If

tree-top accommodation sounds a bit much, there are also bedrooms in the main house.
24560 Monmarves.
Tel: 05 53 27 39 22.
www.chateaugauthie.com

Les Arques
EATING OUT
La Récréation ££
Tucked into an attractive village, this lovely restaurant has become increasingly famous in recent years, both for its chef, Jacques Ratier, and for being the subject of a book by American author Michael Sanders (its title, *You Can't See Paris From Here*, gives you an idea of how deeply set it is in the Lot countryside). A wonderful shady terrace, excellent local produce and friendly service.
46250 Les Arques. Tel: 05 65 22 88 08. Open: Mar–Oct Fri–Wed noon–2pm & 7.30–10pm.

Périgueux
ACCOMMODATION
Ferme de la Maurinie £–££
Around 9km (5½ miles) from the centre of

Périgueux, this working farm has a *chambre d'hôtes*, a campsite and an excellent *auberge*-style restaurant. In their boutique you can buy *foie gras*, *confit de canard* and various other duck products (they offer cooking classes also), and children will love seeing the donkeys and chickens on the farm.
La Maurinie,
24330 Eyliac.
Tel: 05 53 07 57 18.
www.lamaurinie.com

Salles-Monflanquin
ACCOMMODATION
Camping des Bastides £
Well located near to several bastide towns, and ideal for doing the Bastide drive (*see pp114–15*), this has not only standard pitches for tents but the chance to stay in a Mongolian yurt with a wood-burning stove inside – along with beds and bedding. Truly camping without the hassle.
Terre Rouge.
Tel: 05 53 40 83 09.
www. campingdesbastides.com

Sarlat-la-Canéda
ACCOMMODATION
Les Cordeliers £
More of a bed and breakfast than a hotel, this overlooks the Petite Regaudie square in the medieval town centre, and has spacious rooms. Free Wi-Fi and friendly staff make this an excellent-value choice.
51 rue des Cordeliers.
Tel: 05 53 31 94 66.
www.hotelsarlat.com

SPORT AND LEISURE
CycleO
Sarlat is a lovely town to explore by bike, and CycleO is a good place to hire wheels if you want to head off into the (fairly hilly, but very beautiful) surrounding countryside. This place also has outlets in Périgueux. The head office is not at this rental location, so you might want to call ahead and make an appointment to ensure there is someone to greet you.
44 rue des Cordeliers.
Tel: 05 53 31 90 05.
www.cycleo.fr. Open: daily 9am–7pm.

LOT-ET-GARONNE AND LES LANDES

Dax

SPORT AND LEISURE

Les Thermes de l'Avenue
You'll be spoiled for choice when it comes to spas in Dax, but this one offers good day treatments as well as longer stays. Especially recognised for its treatment of arthritis and rheumatism, thanks to the mineral-rich thermal waters. A hotel and restaurant are attached to the spa.
17 avenue Georges Clemenceau. Tel: 05 58 56 35 00. www.thermes-avenue.com

EATING OUT

L'Amphitryon ££
In the hands of the same chef for nearly 20 years, this restaurant serves up dishes that change regularly according to availability and season. The menu leans heavily towards seafood, with a good smattering of some Basque favourites, while the wine list reflects the best of southwest France. Do book ahead – because service hours are short, this place fills up quickly.

38 Cours Gallieni. Tel: 05 58 74 58 05. Open: daily noon– 1pm, 8–9pm.

Duras

ACCOMMODATION

Hostellerie des Ducs ££
Right in the centre of the medieval village of Duras, this lovely hotel and restaurant is well frequented by locals as well as tourists. The bedrooms are a little old-fashioned, but clean and fairly large, and the food in the restaurant is very good quality.

The Hostellerie des Ducs is also one of the most popular 'destination' restaurants (*Open: daily 12.30–1.30pm & 7.30– 9.15pm*) in Duras (meaning that it's where locals take their friends when they come to stay) and concentrates on plentiful portions of regional classics. Choose from the fixed-price menu or treat yourself to more elaborate à la carte dishes.
Boulevard Jean-Brisseau. Tel: 05 53 83 74 58. www.hostellerieducs-duras.com

Eugénie-les-Bains

ACCOMMODATION

Les Prés d'Eugénie ££££
One of the best-known hotels in Les Landes (and the whole of southwest France), Les Prés is owned by renowned chef Michel Guérard. This place is all about relaxation, pampering yourself, enjoying the beautiful surroundings… and eating as often as you can. Set in this pretty spa town between Mont-de-Marsan and Aire-sur-l'Adour, the hotel gives very easy access to the attractions of both places (if you ever want to leave the pool-side).
40320 Eugénie-les-Bains. Tel: 05 58 05 05 05. www.michelguerard.com

Léon

ACCOMMODATION

Camping Lou Puntaou £
Two minutes' walk from Léon's beautiful lake and in the middle of the Huchet nature reserve. The ocean is just 6km (4 miles) away, so you are never going to be short of things to do. The campsite itself is well equipped with a pool, a

good shop and plenty of games, but the best thing is the site's proximity to the boating, swimming, canoeing and cycling opportunities all around.
1315 avenue du Lac. Tel: 05 58 48 74 30. www.loupuntaou.com

Moirax
Eating out
Auberge du Prieuré ££
It may not be easy to find, hidden in a tiny village in the Lot-et-Garonne, but it boasts some pretty special food, thanks to chef Benjamin Toursel.
Le Bourg. Tel: 05 53 47 59 55. www.aubergeduprieurede moirax.fr. Open: Wed–Sun 12.30–2pm & 8–9.30pm.

Mont-de-Marsan
Eating out
Un Air de Campagne ££
A slightly formal setting, but very good food at this well-located restaurant. Plenty of regional produce.
3 rue Thèses Claire. Tel: 05 58 06 05 41. www.un-air-de-campagne.com

Sabres
Accommodation
Auberge des Pins ££
This is easily one of the best places to stay in the area, set in the heart of Les Landes regional park. It offers a beautiful traditional building, with plenty of dark wood and exposed beams, and well-sized, impeccably decorated rooms. There is a very good restaurant, and bedrooms have flat-screen TVs and free Wi-Fi (but all so subtle you barely notice the modern conveniences). And the price is incredible – just one of the benefits of travelling to the less well-known parts of France!
40630 Sabres. Tel: 05 58 08 30 00. Email: contact@ aubergedespins.fr. www.aubergedespins.fr

Eating out
La Table de Marquèze ££
It's worth a trip to the excellent Écomusée de Marquèze for this restaurant alone. Set among pine trees, with wooden tables outside on the terrace, you feel healthy just sitting down here, never mind ordering the plentiful fresh food of the region. Book ahead, even if it's just when you arrive, as a small train takes you to the restaurant, and if there are a lot of people, you might find it hard to get a prime outside spot.
40630 Sabres. Tel: 05 58 07 59 44. www.parc-landes-de-gascogne.fr

Saint-Julien-en-Born
Sport and leisure
Jungle Park
A tree-top adventure park in Les Landes that has four separate circuits for different ages and abilities. One of the biggest in southwest France, with a paintball centre next door.
D41 route de Contis. Tel: 06 32 65 16 81.

Saint-Michel-Escalus
Sport and leisure
Canoe Land
A well-equipped canoe centre with good training for beginners and families. You can take out single kayaks, or canoes for up to four people.
235 route de Linxe. Tel: 05 58 72 61 78. Admission charge.

Index

Acknowledgements

Thomas Cook Publishing wishes to thank NICHOLAS INMAN, to whom the copyright belongs, for the photographs in this book, except for the following images:

CRTMP page 149 (D Viet); DREAMSTIME.COM pages 16 (Gregory Guivarch), 29 (Anna Baburkina), 30 (Andrew Emptage), 31 (Cafaphotos), 35 (Anibal Trejo), 37 (Mermozine), 55 (Frank Farrell), 56 (Olga Topp), 59 (Oleg Mitiukhin), 69 (Jarnogz), 72 (Álvaro Germán Vilela), 82 (Yvon52), 84 (Cynoclub), 99 (Hartemink), 111 (Elena Elisseeva), 113 (David Taylor-Hughes), 115 (Davidmartyn), 133 (Benjamin Guillemet); OT TOULOUSE page 157 (F Dumond); VILLE DE TOULOUSE pages 11, 25, 148, 152, 161 (Patrice Nin), 94, 154 (José Manuel Herrador), 163 (Manuel Huynh), 91; WIKIMEDIA COMMONS pages 43 (Chell Hill), 57, 83 (Larrousiney), 61, 129, 130 (Jibi44), 85 (Robespierre), 109 (HTO), 127, 128 (Claus Thoemmes), 166 (Nils Oberg).

For CAMBRIDGE PUBLISHING MANAGEMENT LIMITED:
Project editor: Tom Lee
Copy editor: Anne McGregor
Typesetter: Trevor Double
Proofreaders: Penelope Kent & Jan McCann
Indexer: Marie Lorimer

SEND YOUR THOUGHTS TO
BOOKS@THOMASCOOK.COM

We're committed to providing the very best up-to-date information in our travel guides and constantly strive to make them as useful as they can be. You can help us to improve future editions by letting us have your feedback. If you've made a wonderful discovery on your travels that we don't already feature, if you'd like to inform us about recent changes to anything that we do include, or if you simply want to let us know your thoughts about this guidebook and how we can make it even better – we'd love to hear from you.

Send us ideas, discoveries and recommendations today and then look out for your valuable input in the next edition of this title.

Emails to the above address, or letters to the traveller guides Series Editor, Thomas Cook Publishing, PO Box 227, Coningsby Road, Peterborough PE3 8SB, UK.

Please don't forget to let us know which title your feedback refers to!